A YOUNG UNITARIAN UNIVERSALIST'S

DOODLE·OGRAPHY JOURNAL

Created by

with a little help from **LINDY GIFFORD**

Don't forget to doodle on this page.

A Young Unitarian Universalist's Doodle-ography Journal
Perfect bound edition ©2020 Lindy Gifford
ISBN 978-1-7322068-2-3

Illustrations, hand lettering, and book design by Lindy Gifford
Published by Doodle-ography, an imprint of Unorthodox Books
www.doodle-ography.com

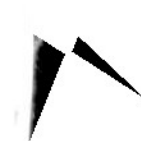

Did you know doodling is good for you? Some people seem to think that when you are doodling you are not paying attention. But as anyone who doodles already knows, that's not true. Doodling actually helps you remember things you hear. And it's very relaxing. It can calm you down if you are feeling upset or bored. Your Doodle-ography Journal can also help you learn about Unitarian Universalism in a new way.

Doodle-ography is easy and fun. You have probably doodled before—maybe you doodle all the time. Doodle-ography is a lot like that, but a little different. Try this: Draw patterns and shapes, instead of pictures of things. If you do draw a thing, try filling it up with patterns! Don't think too much or plan how you want your doodles to look. Work quickly if that feels right, or draw the line slowly and calmly and just watch it appear behind your pen—as if by magic.

This is a quiet adventure. (Yes, there is such a thing.) While you doodle, listen. If no one is speaking, listen to sounds around you. Listen to your breath. And most of all, listen to the still, small voice inside you. That is what will guide where the doodles go. You might even find that they take on a life of their own. It can be very exciting to see what happens each time you sit down with your journal!

Start on whichever page feels right. If you're not sure, try starting with one of the pages that has an outline divided into sections. Fill each section with a different pattern. (Doodle on the page outside the picture, too!) Some pages have words to read and doodle around, as you think about them. The backs of the printed pages are blank, so ink won't go through onto another outline or quote. If you'd rather doodle on a blank page, just use the back!

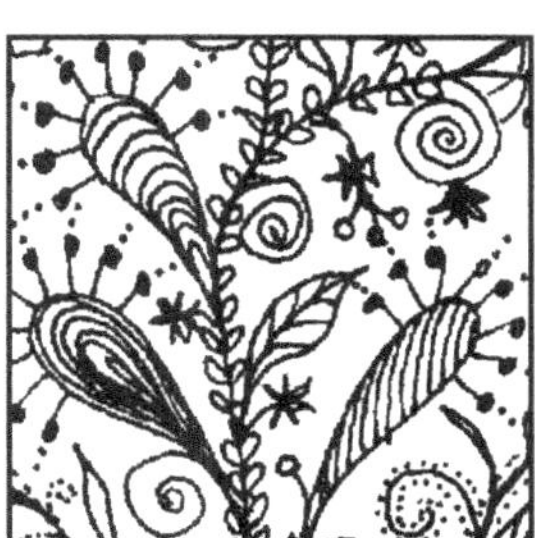

This is not really a coloring book. This is a better doodling book than it is a coloring book—until *you* make it into a coloring book. Think of it as decorating the images with patterns and lines, rather than coloring them in. You can use black or colored pens or markers. Then if you like coloring, you can color the spaces you have made with your doodles. In that way, you can make this journal into your own, really good, coloring book.

Be kind. To yourself and others. Please don't compare journals or comment to others on their doodles or yours. Your journal will be unlike anyone else's, a unique expression of who you are. There is no wrong way to do this, but if you feel as if you have "messed up," try to keep going anyway. Sometimes what we think of as a mistake can be a special gift in disguise. If it still doesn't feel right, leave that page for now and go to another. But try coming back to it another time. You just might find something surprising there.

Words work, too. If you hear words you want to remember, write them in your journal and make them a part of your doodles. If you are thinking about someone, write that person's name and draw a doodled prayer around it. Or write down your own words, perhaps a poem, and decorate them. But most important: keep doodling and have fun!

Enjoy the adventure!

What Doodle-ography can do. It can calm and center children (and adults!) on a very deep level. It is also being used very successfully as a support for attentive listening during story times and services. Doodling can be an effective aid to increase focus for children who struggle with attention and anxiety issues. Visual learners and children who already doodle are instantly drawn to the journal, but even those who are self-conscious about their artistic abilities find their creativity blossoms in the non-threatening context of the Doodle-ography Journal.

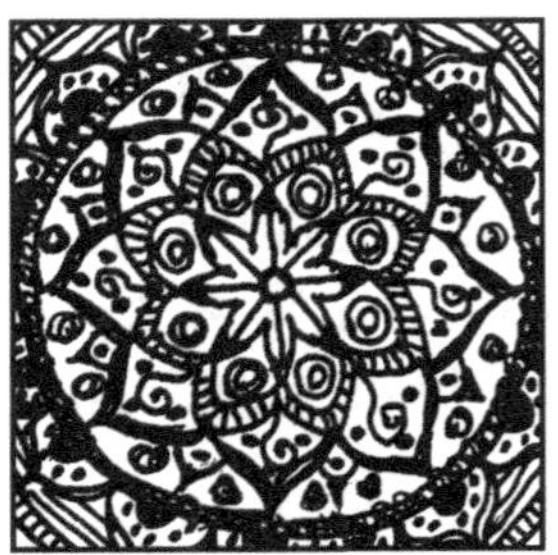

Doodling to focus and calm the mind. Research shows that people who doodle while listening retain up to 29% more information than those who do not.* By quieting the chatter of the mind, doodling in this journal can also become a beautiful visual and tactile meditation practice, especially accessible to children. The images and prompts gently introduce and reinforce Unitarian Universalist teachings, as well as those of other world traditions, wise women and men, and the earth.

Doodle-ography is a way to connect with Spirit. Small children connect naturally with life and themselves through uncensored artistic expression. Sadly, as they grow they are often told that art is not important, or that they are not "good" at it. Doodle-ography is an easy, nonthreatening way to help reestablish and nurture that connection. Through use of this journal, they can also rediscover their birthright connection to Spirit.

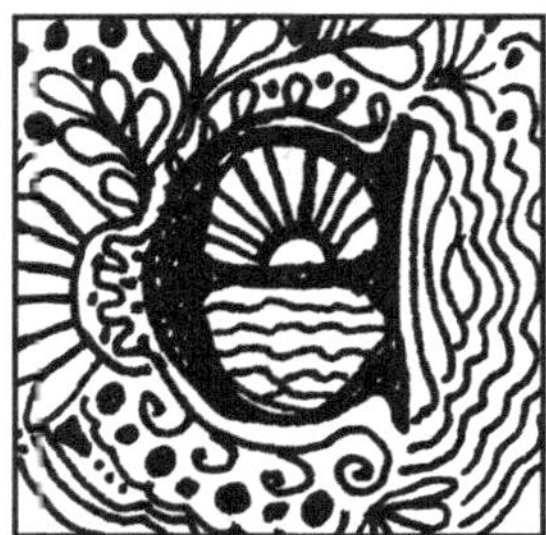

Creating art in this way is both ancient and sacred. Once, all art was "sacred art." The oldest art, cave painting, was ritual art created far from "public view" and often overlapped, obscuring the images. Native American and Tibetan sand painting are other examples of sacred art where the focus is on the act of creation, rather than on a final product. Like all these sacred art forms, Doodle-ography taps into something profound and universal.

How to use the journal in class and church. Keep the journals and pens at church to use during Sunday services, religious education classes, Coming of Age programs, and youth groups. Older kids "get" doodling easily and especially love gel pens. Younger children enjoy filling the pages in their own way with age-appropriate markers or crayons. In services, the journals naturally calm and quiet children. Unlike common fidget toys, they also actively connect them with their faith. And eventually each child will have created a personal visual record of his or her journey and a memento of our faith community to take home and keep.

Giving guidance. Everyone benefits from some guidance when getting started and reading together the "Getting Started" section can help. But it is also important not to over-guide, and always ask permission to see a child's journal. Never tell a child they are not doing it right. Because there is actually no right way, and ultimately everyone will find their own way. For more information and help getting started: **doodle-ography.com.**

P.S. Doodling is good for adults, too! I always model focused doodling, and doodle along.

* J.Andrade, "What does doodling do?" *Applied Cognitive Psychology* (2010) Volume 24, pp. 100-106.

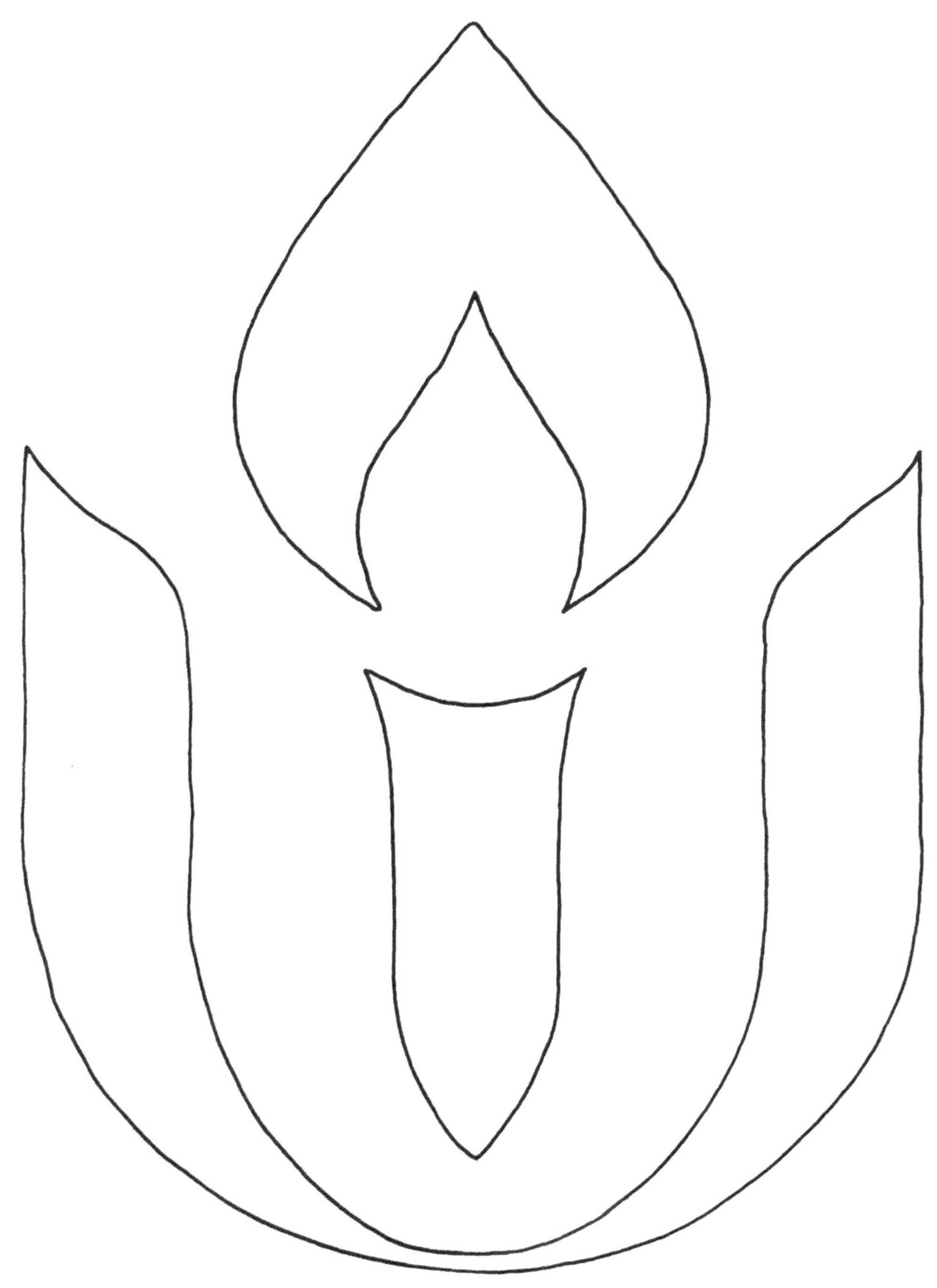

We, the member congregations of
the Unitarian Universalist Association,
covenant to affirm and promote...

The seven principles of our living tradition:

1

The inherent worth and dignity
of every person...

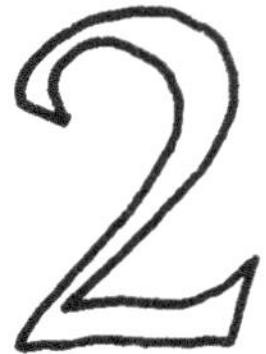 Justice, equity and compassion
in human relations...

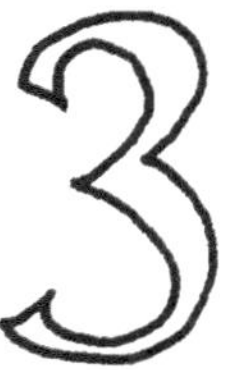 Acceptance of one another
and encouragement to spiritual
growth in our congregations...

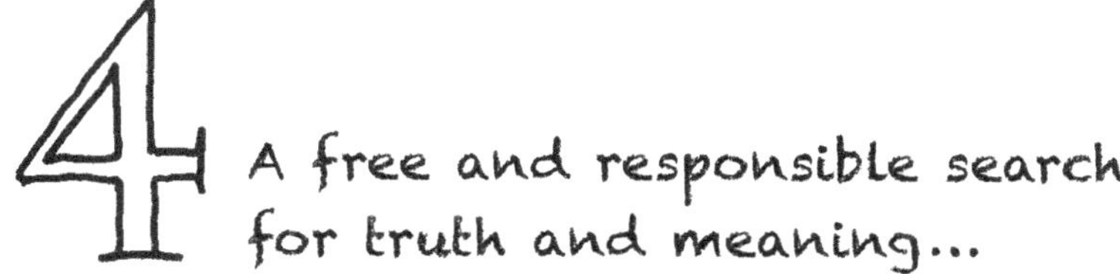

A free and responsible search
for truth and meaning...

The right of conscience and the use
of the democratic process within our
congregations and in society at large...

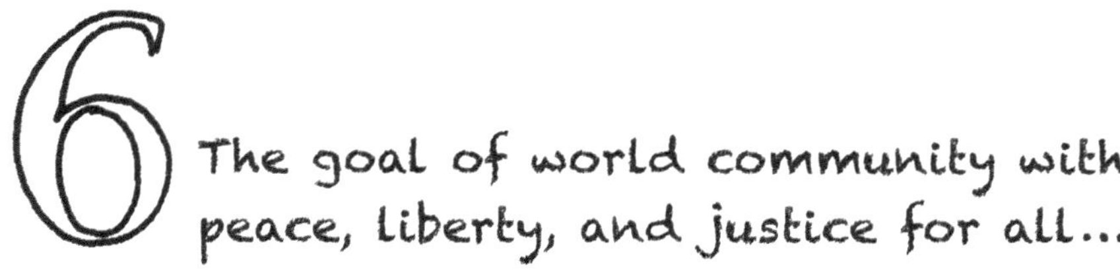

6 The goal of world community with peace, liberty, and justice for all…

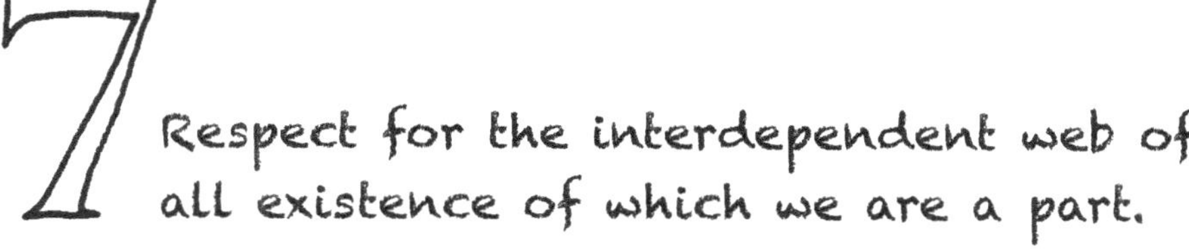

7 Respect for the interdependent web of
all existence of which we are a part.

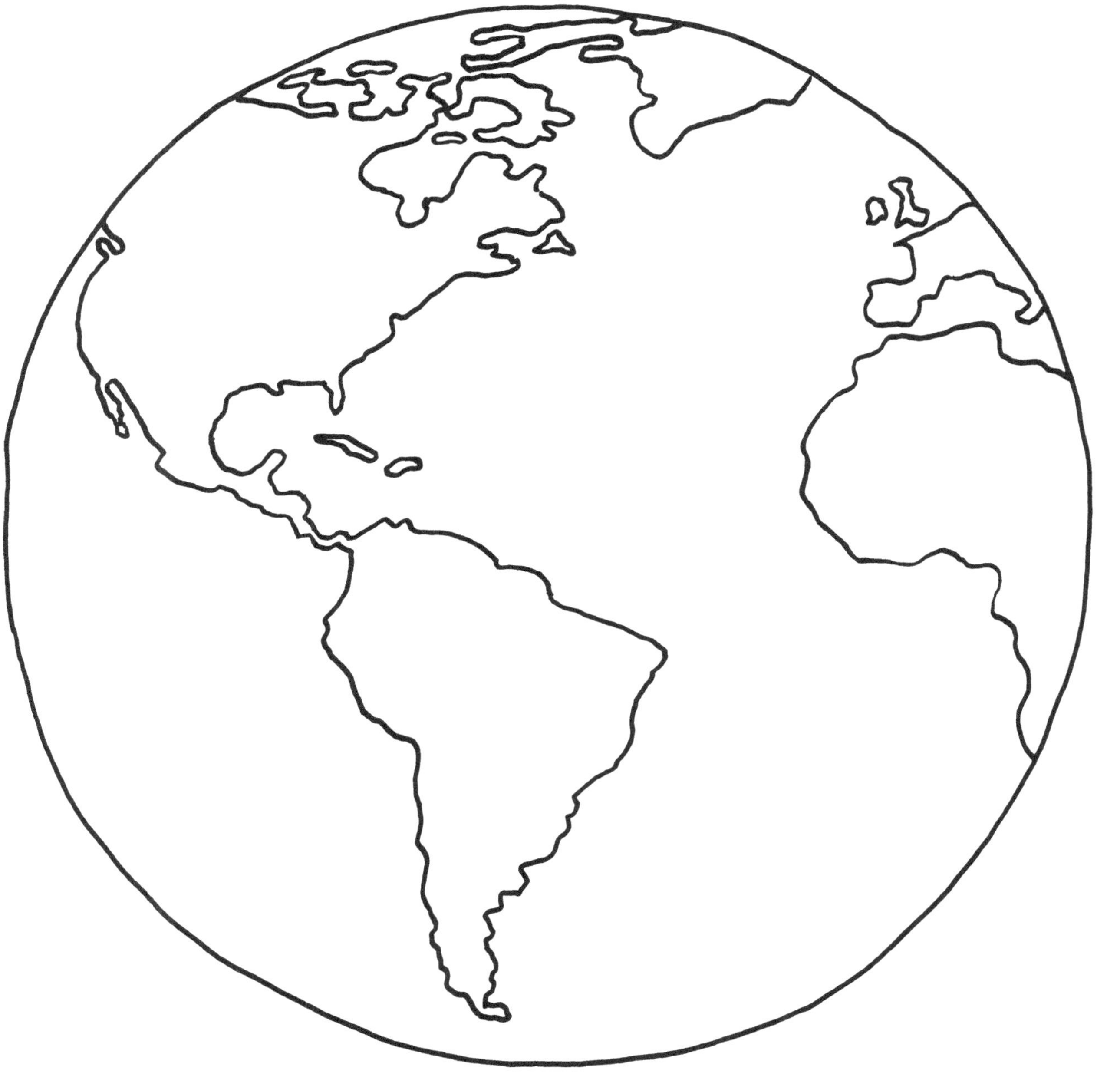

The six sources of our living tradition:

1 Direct experience of that transcending mystery and wonder, affirmed in all cultures, which moves us to a renewal of the spirit and an openness to the forces which create and uphold life...

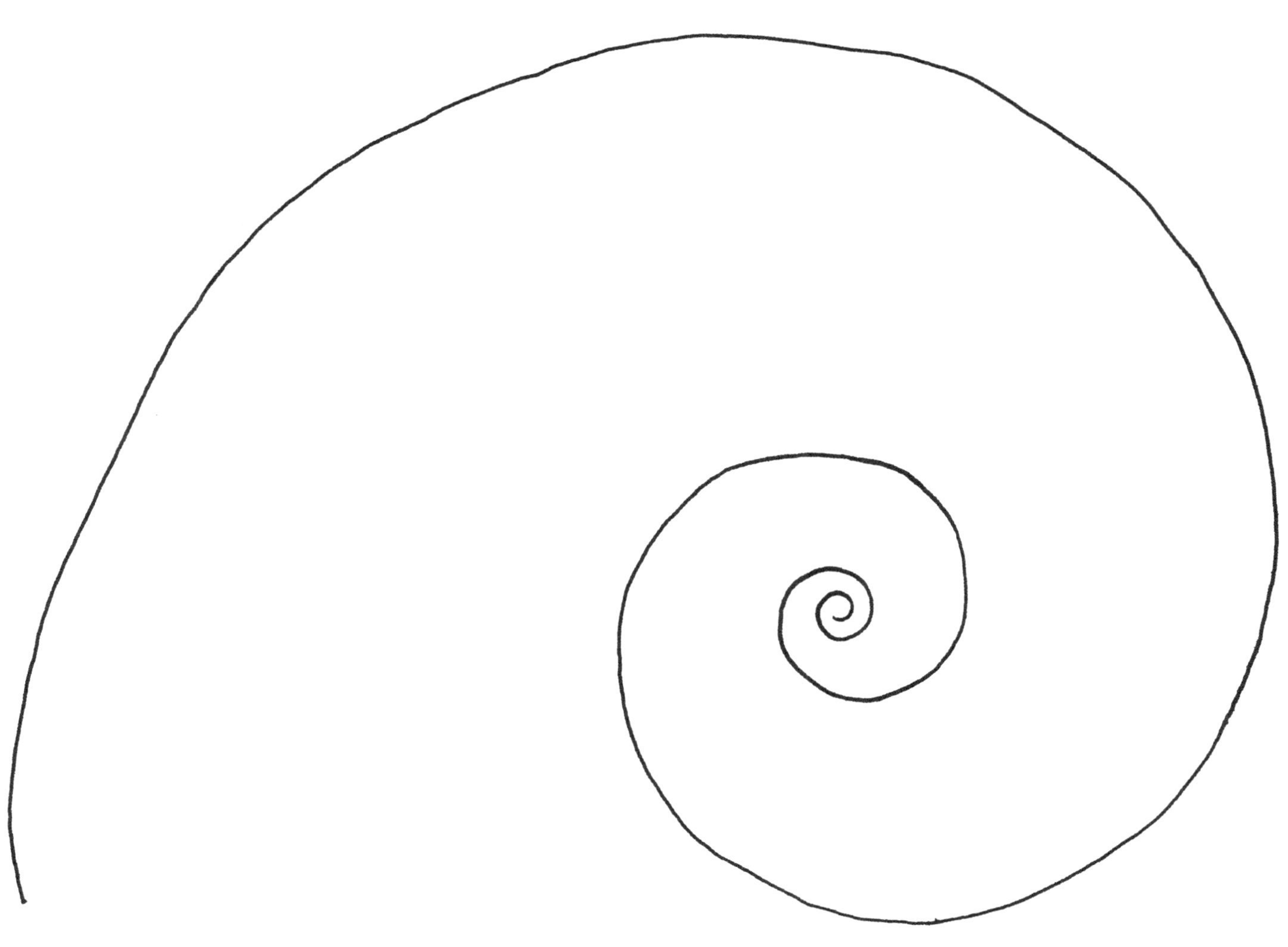

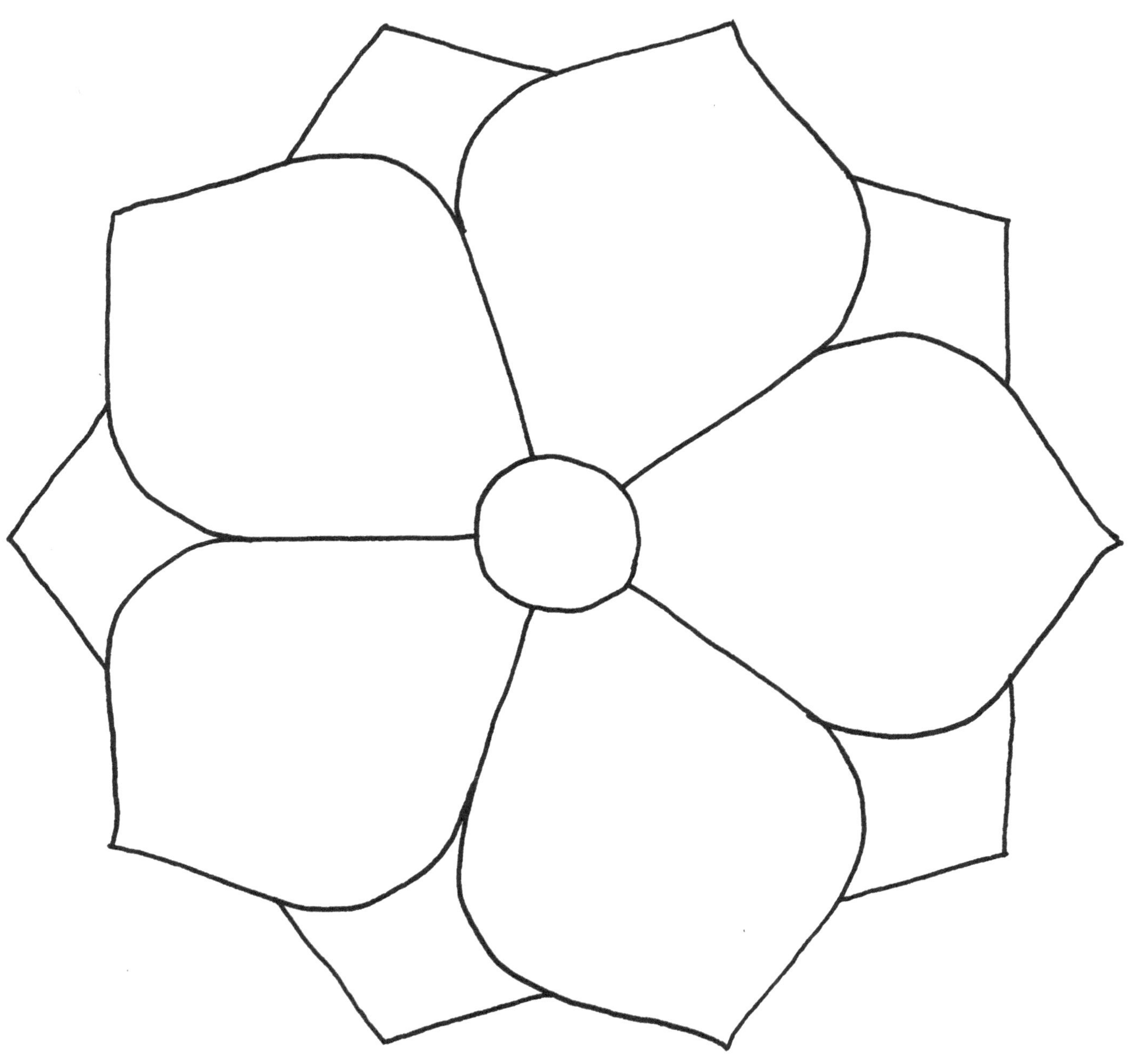

2

Words and deeds of prophetic women and men which challenge us to confront powers and structures of evil with justice, compassion, and the transforming power of love...

Resistance to tyranny
is obedience to God.

Susan B. Anthony

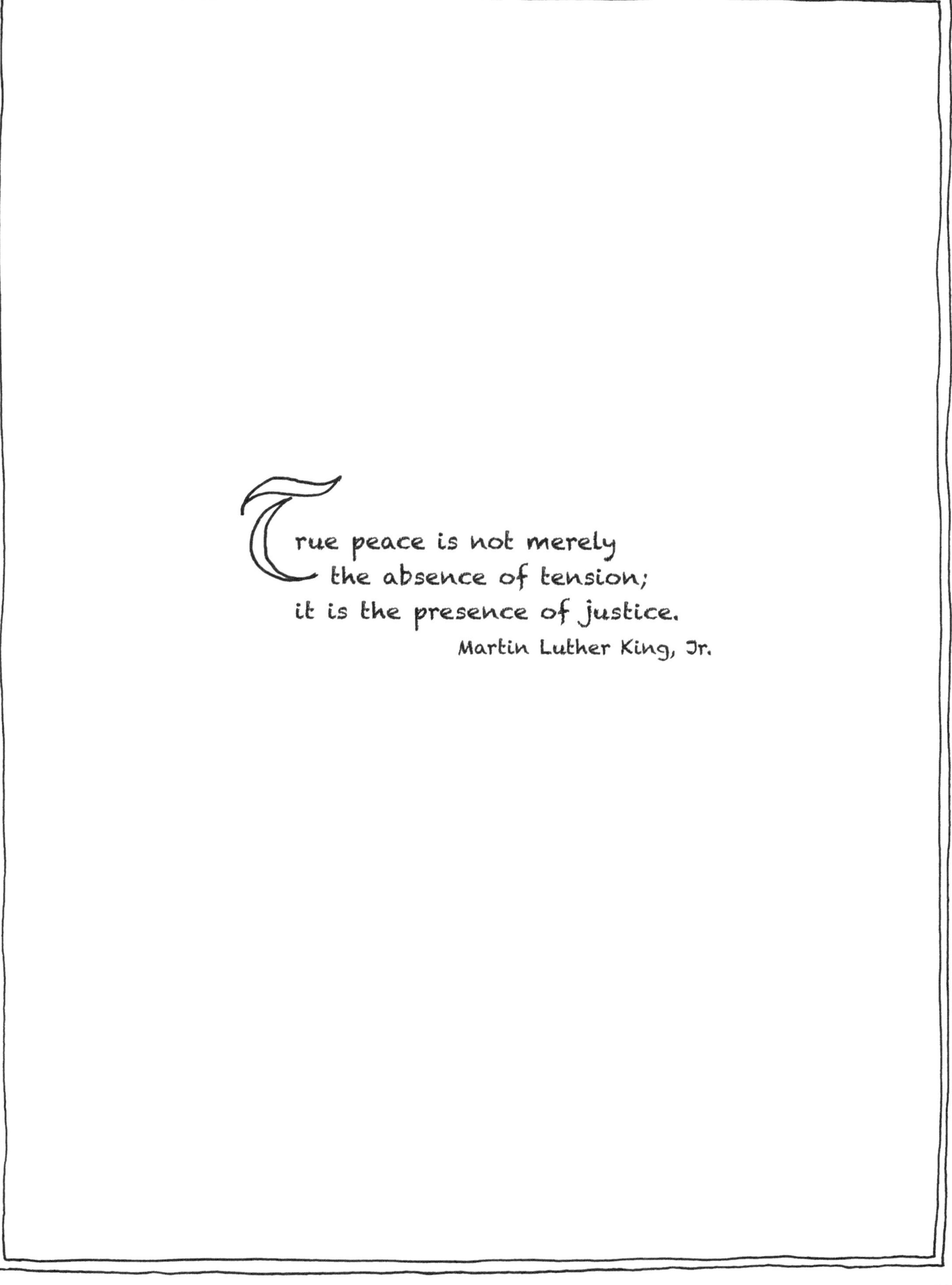

True peace is not merely
the absence of tension;
it is the presence of justice.
Martin Luther King, Jr.

Religions are different roads converging to the same point. What does it matter that we take different roads, so long as we reach the same goal. Wherein is the cause for quarreling?

Mahatma Gandhi

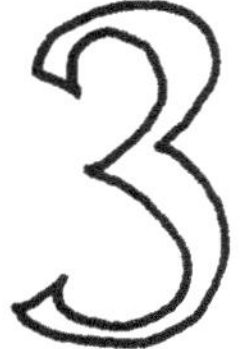

3
Wisdom from the world's religions which inspires us in our ethical and spiritual life...

Islam

If you do deeds of charity openly, it is well; but if you bestow it upon the needy in secret, it will be even better.

The Koran

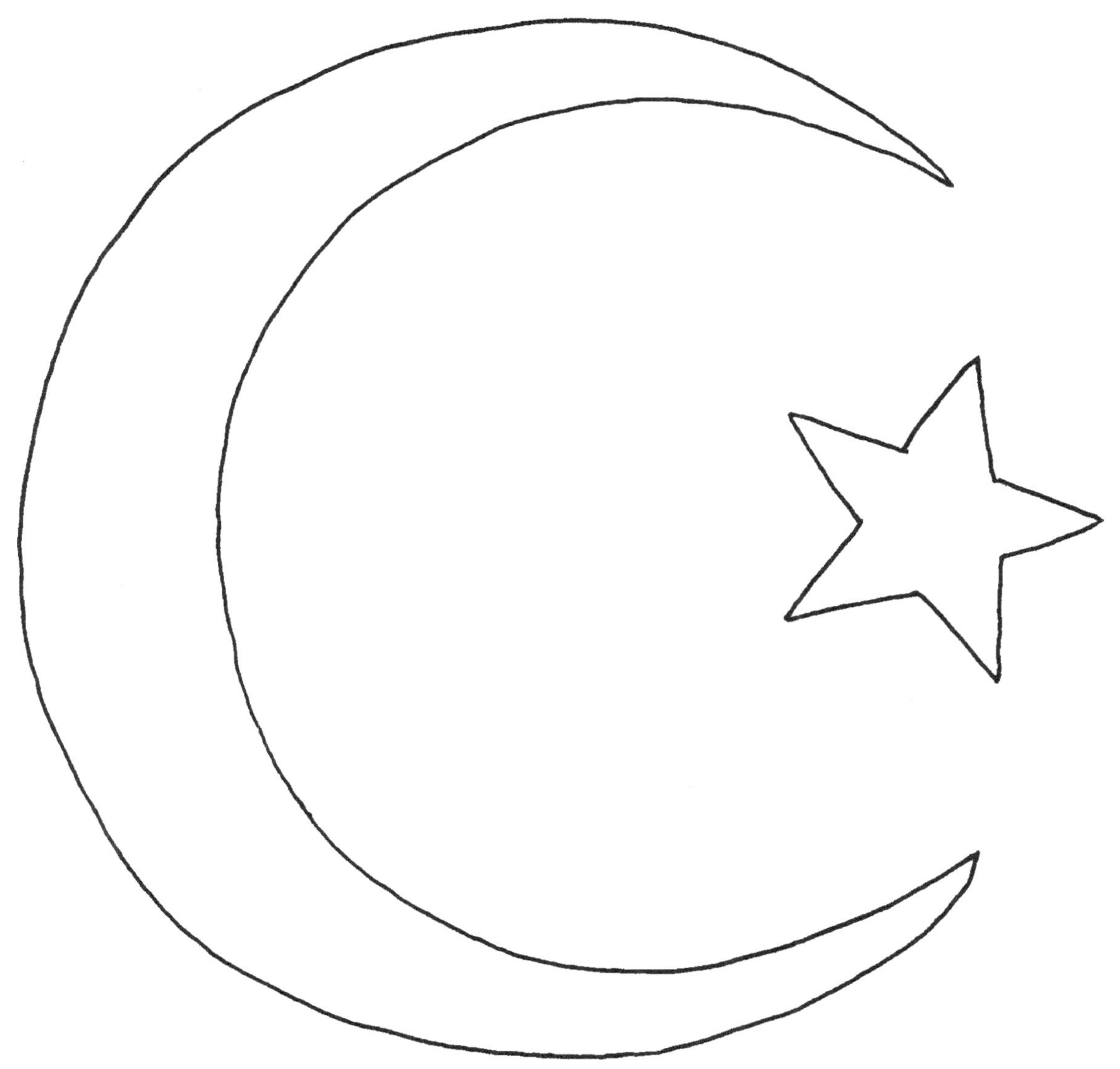

Drop by drop is the water pot filled.
Likewise, the wise man, gathering it little
by little, fills himself with good.

The Buddha

Buddhism

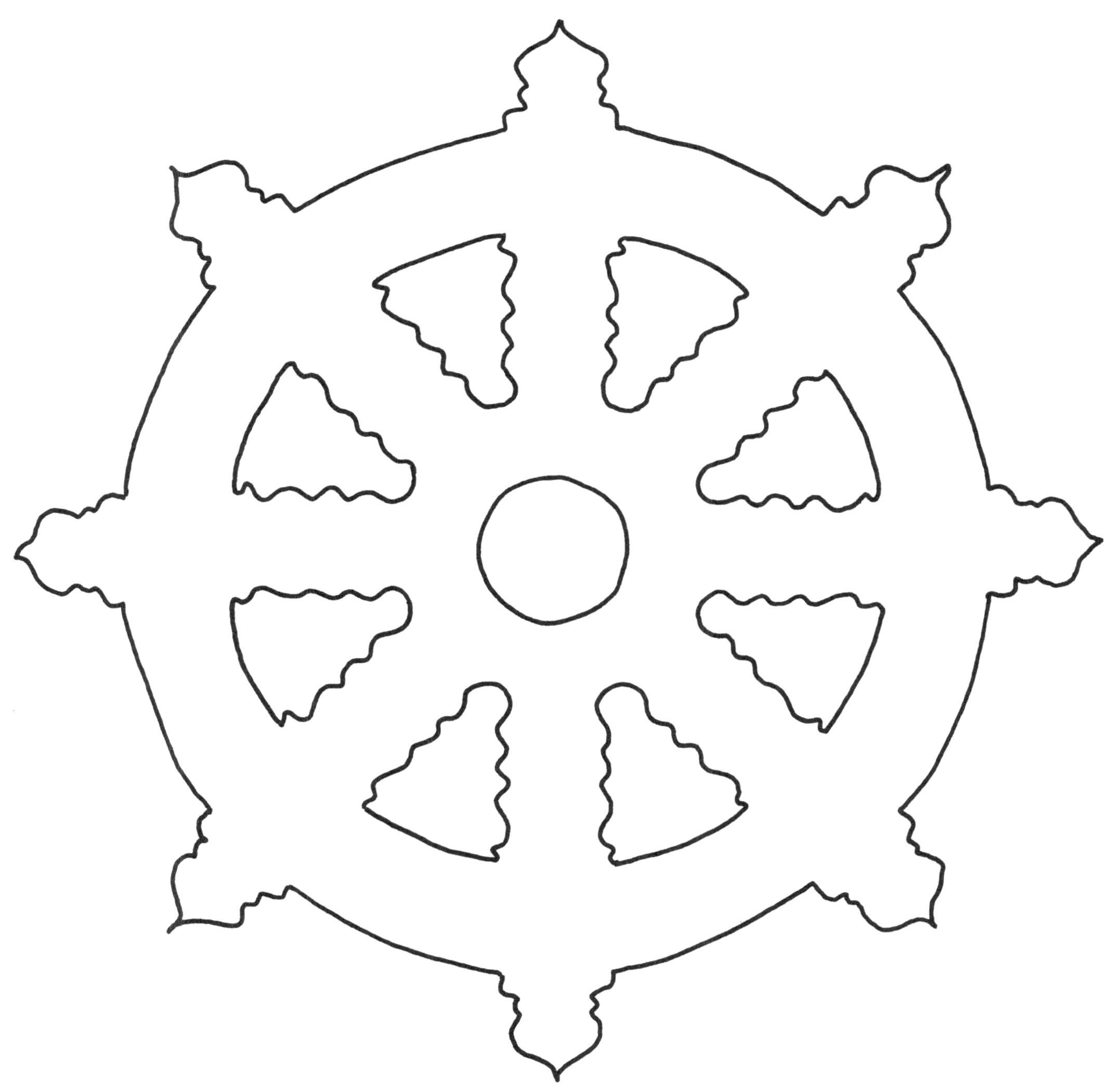

Truth is one. Sages call it by different names.

Rig Veda

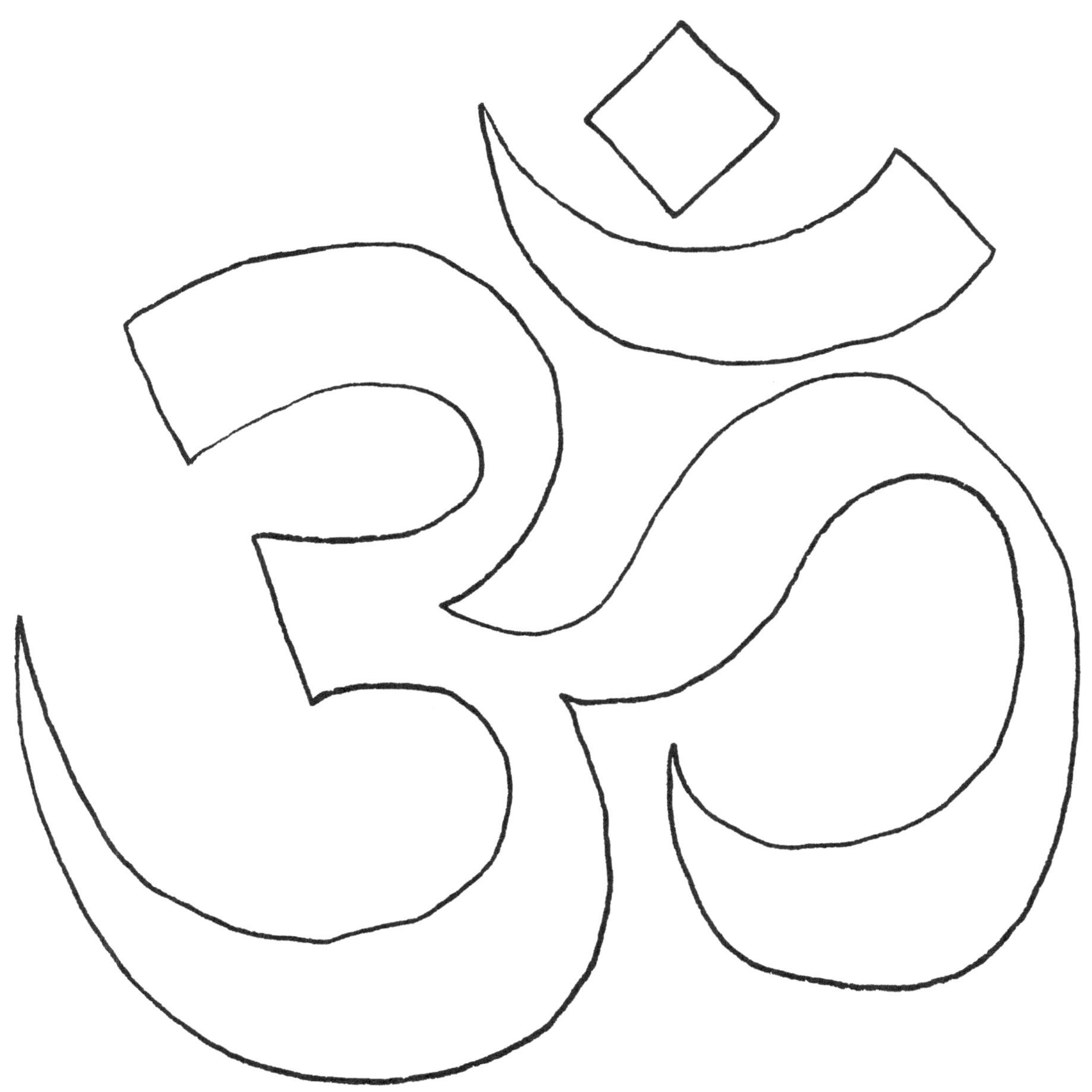

Give a man a fish and you feed him for a day. Teach him how to fish and you feed him for a lifetime.

Lao-Tzu

YANG
light
sun
masculine
brightness
activity
east
south
sky
energy

YIN
darkness
moon
feminine
shade
rest
west
north
earth
matter

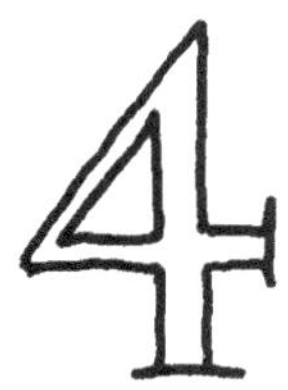 Jewish and Christian teachings which call us to respond
to God's love by loving our neighbors as ourselves...

Judaism

What is hateful to you,
do not do to your fellowman.
This is the entire Law;
all the rest is commentary.

Talmud, Shabbat 3id

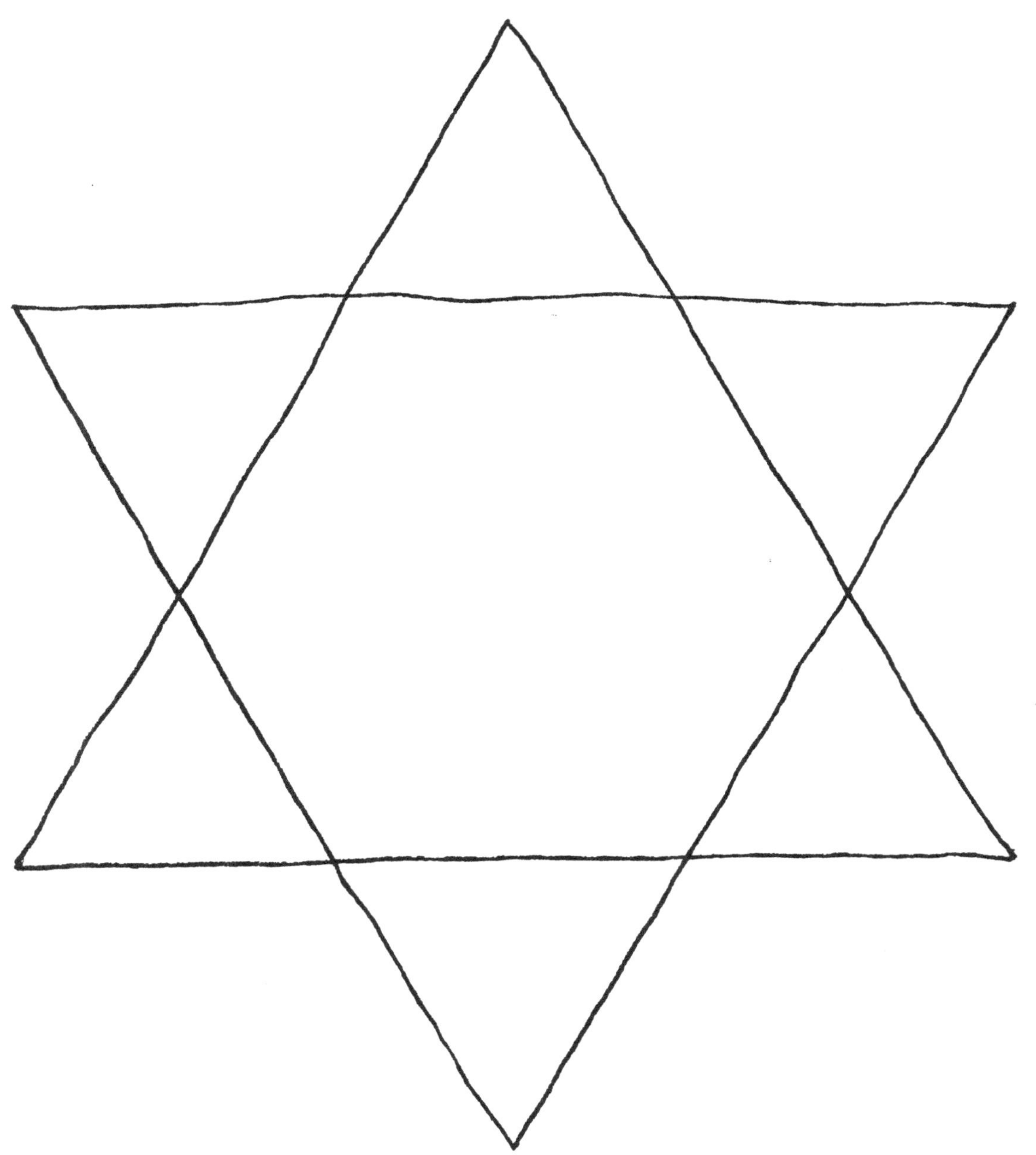

All things whatsoever ye would
that men should do to you,
do ye so to them; for this is
the law and the prophets.

Matthew 7:1

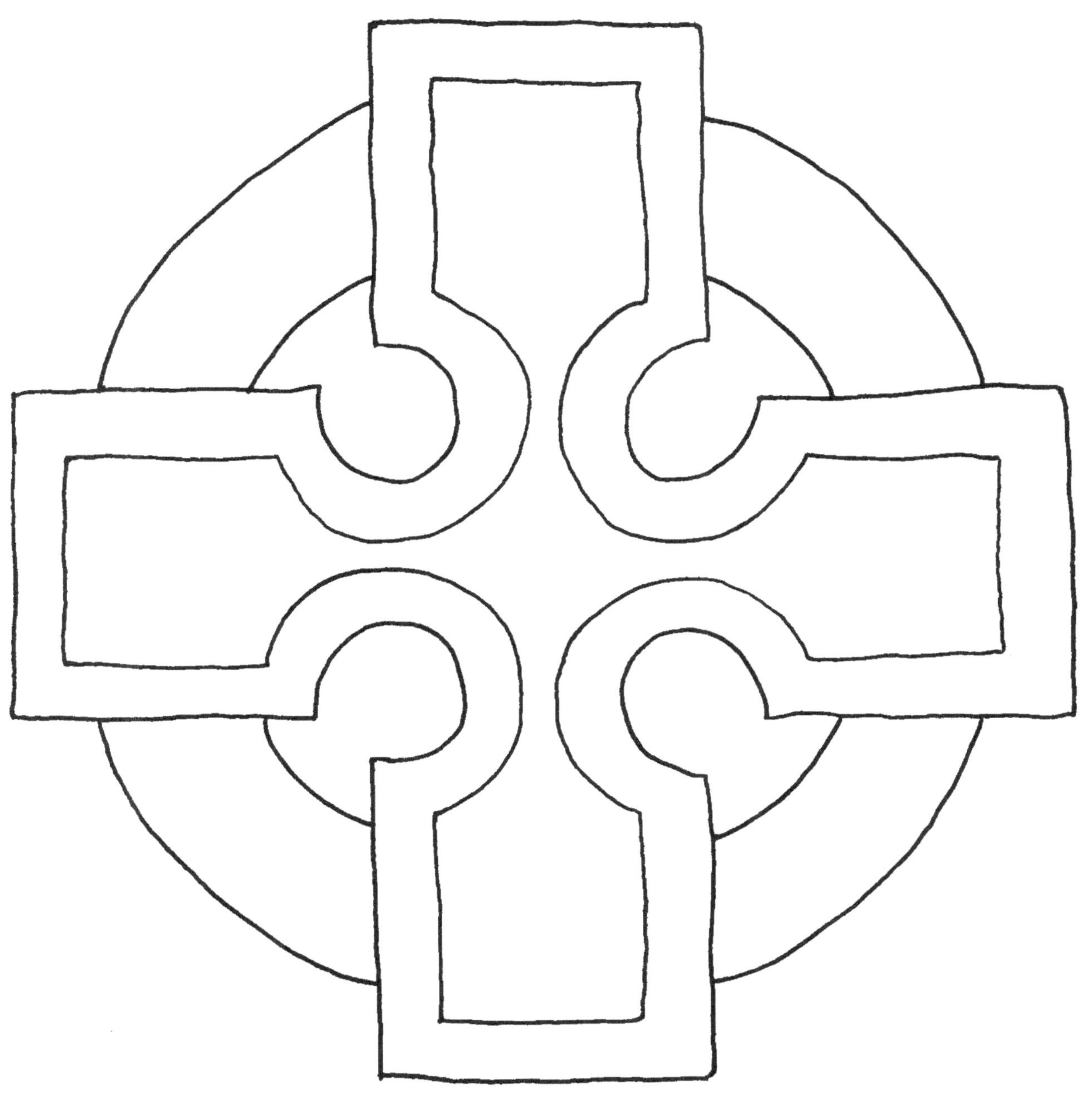

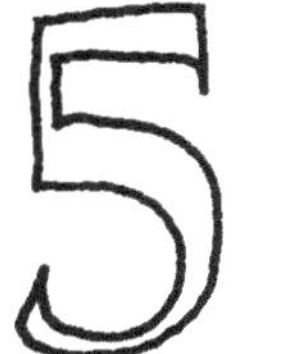

Humanist teachings which counsel us to heed the guidance of reason and the results of science, and warn us against idolatries of the mind and spirit...

The deeper we look into nature, the more we recognize that it is full of life, and the more profoundly we know that all life is a secret and that we are united with all life that is in nature.

Albert Schweitzer

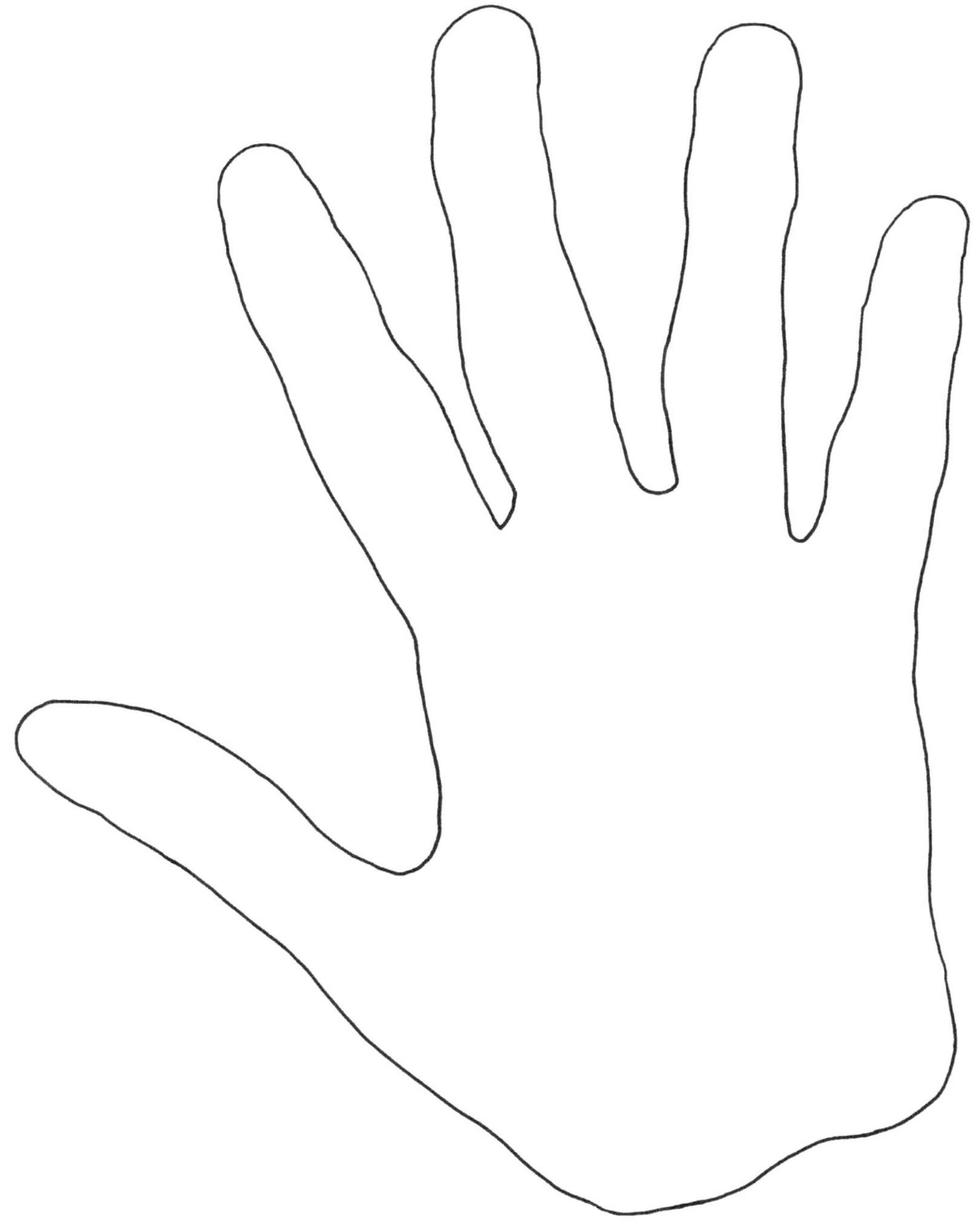

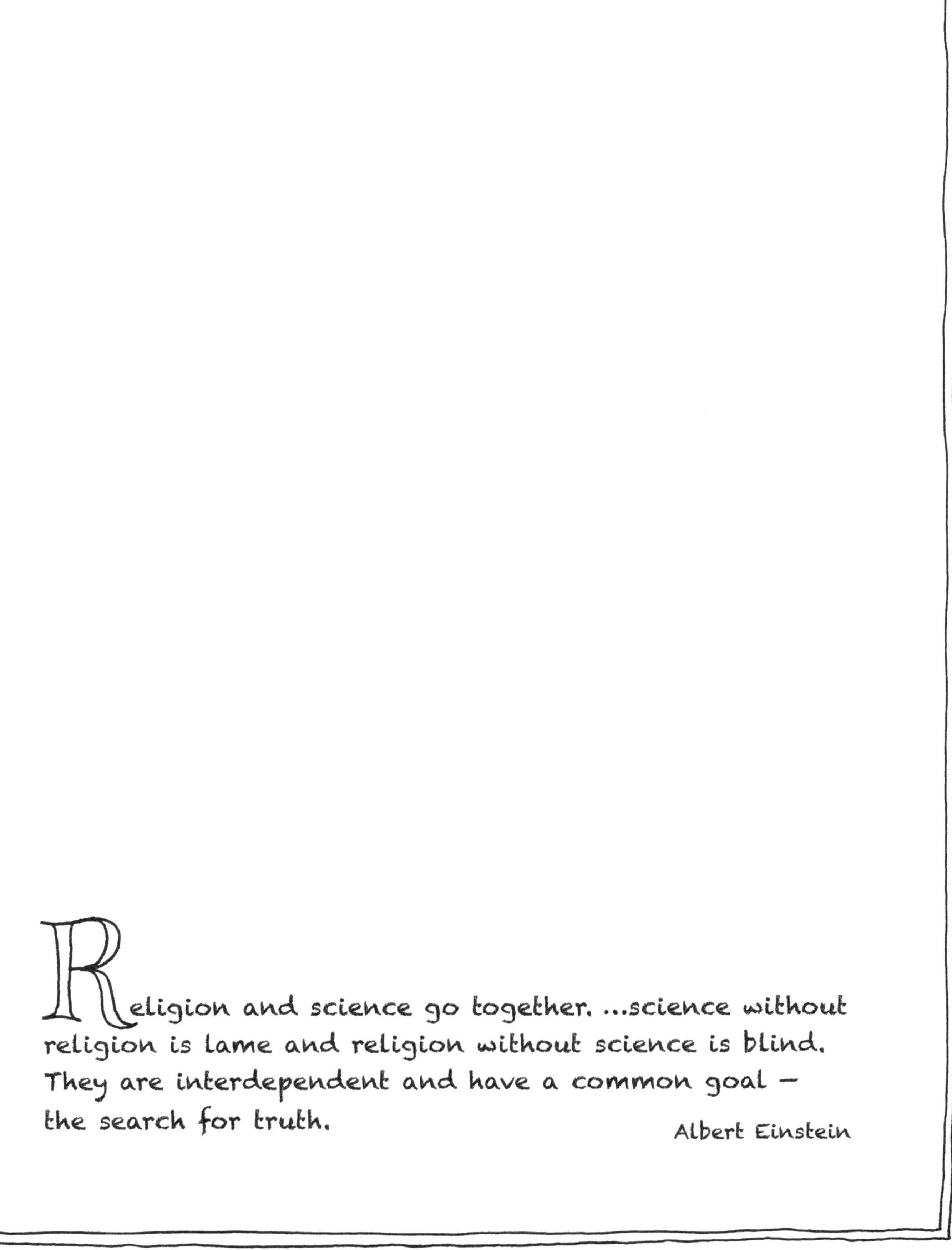

Religion and science go together. ...science without religion is lame and religion without science is blind. They are interdependent and have a common goal — the search for truth.

Albert Einstein

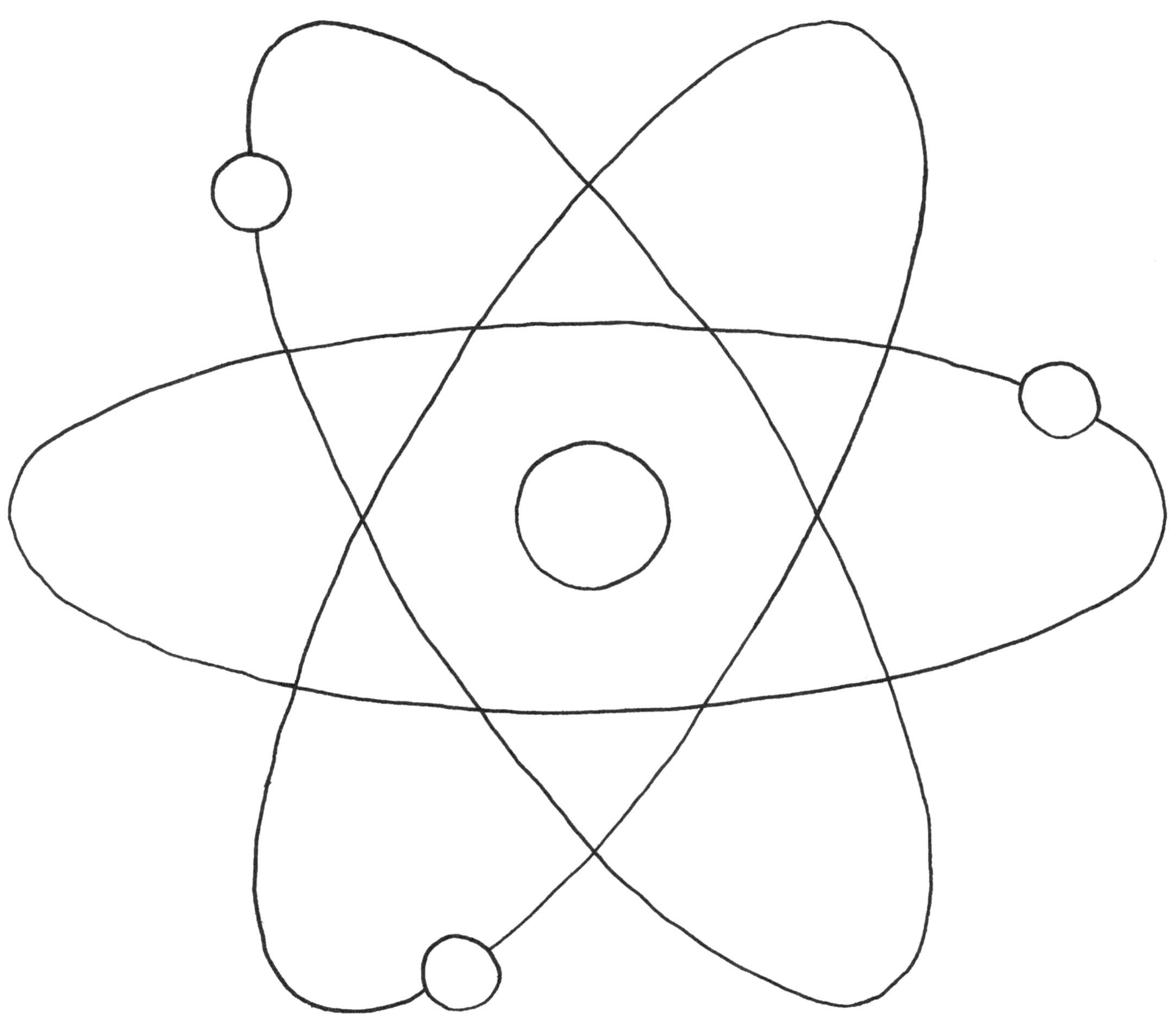

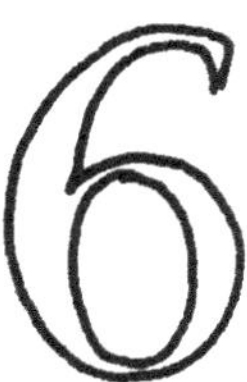

Spiritual teachings of earth-centered traditions which celebrate the sacred circle of life and instruct us to live in harmony with the rhythms of nature...

Deep peace of the running wave to you.
Deep peace of the flowing air to you.
Deep peace of the quiet earth to you.
Deep peace of the shining stars to you.
Deep peace of the infinite peace to you.

Gaelic blessing

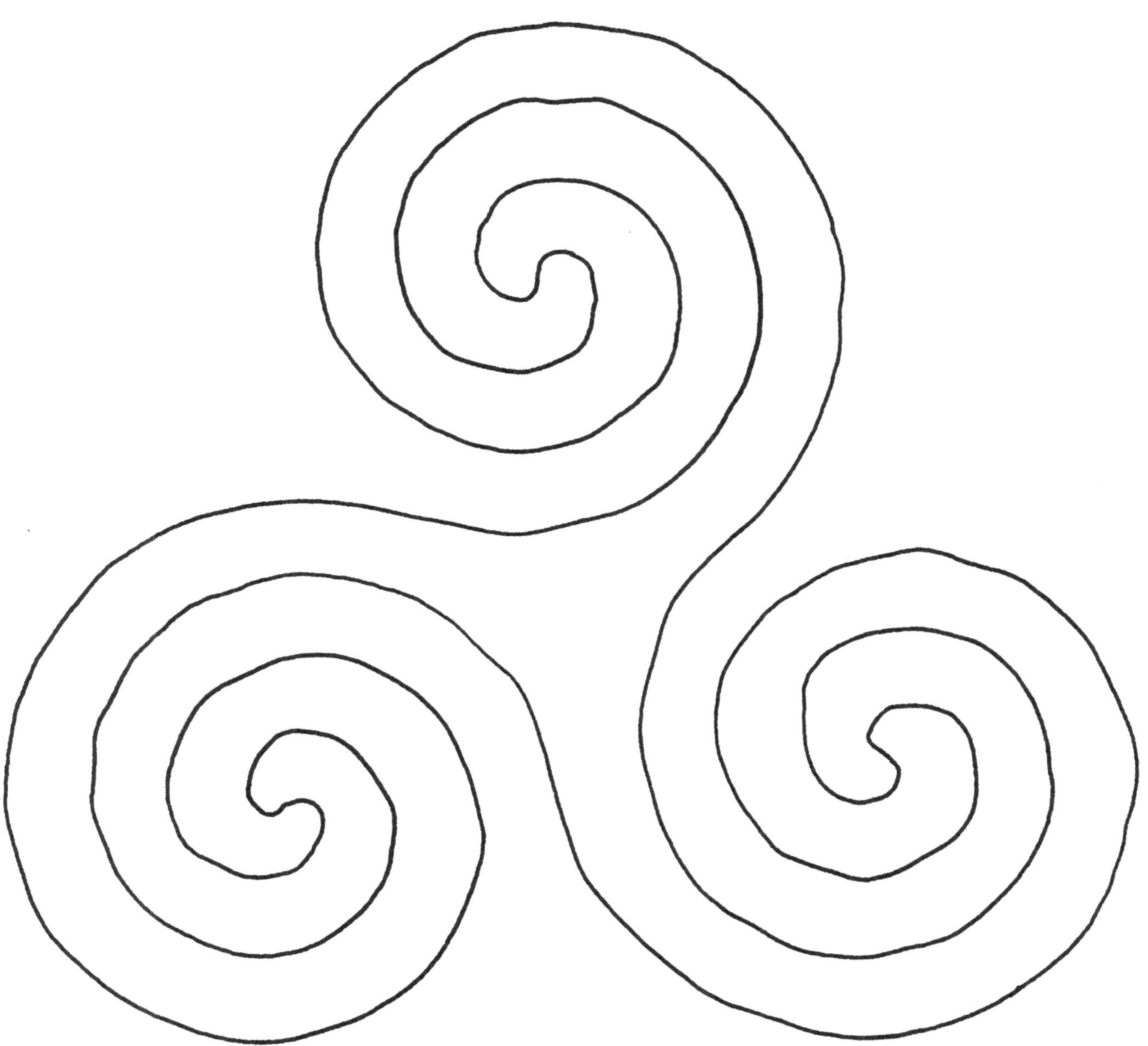

59

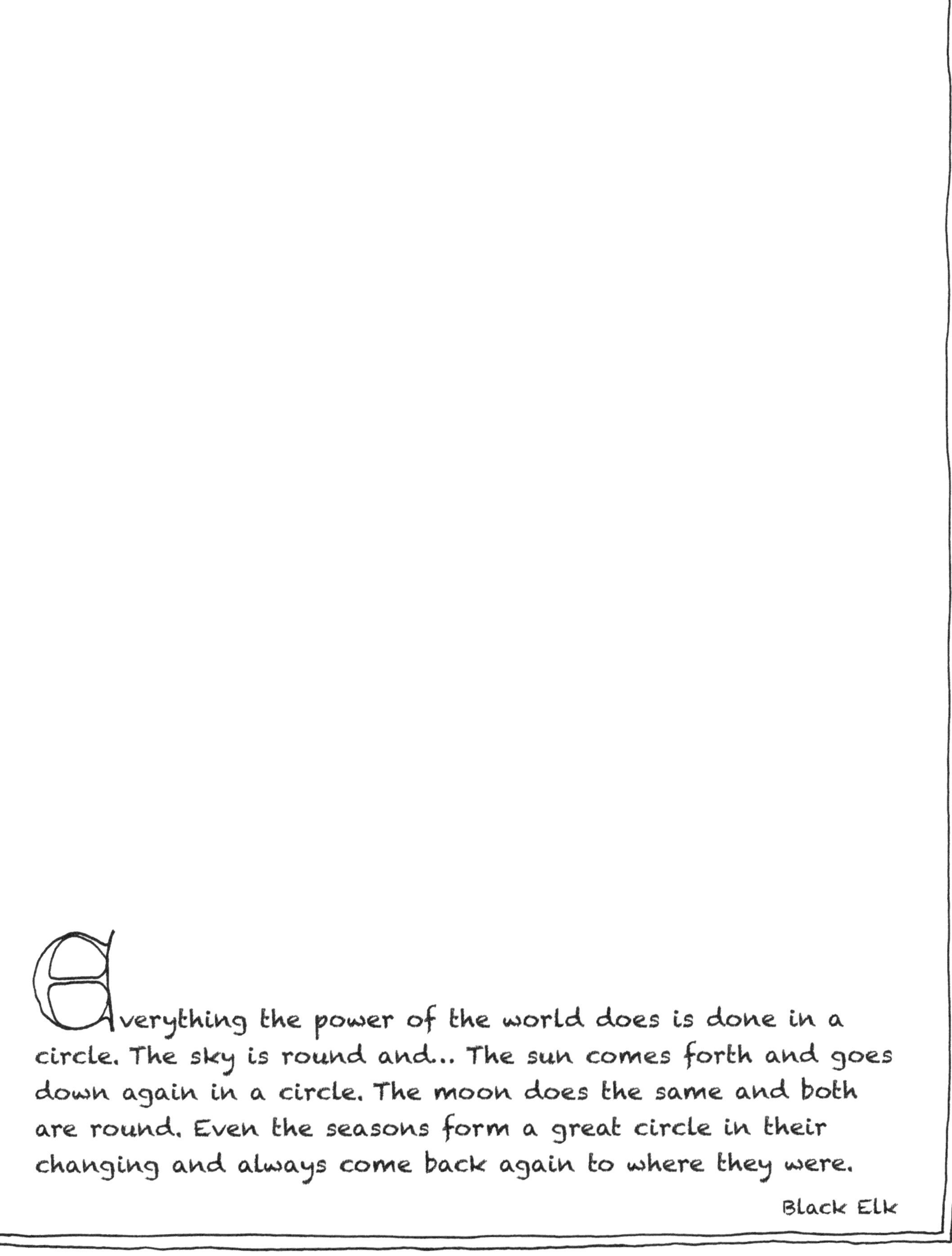

Everything the power of the world does is done in a circle. The sky is round and... The sun comes forth and goes down again in a circle. The moon does the same and both are round. Even the seasons form a great circle in their changing and always come back again to where they were.

Black Elk

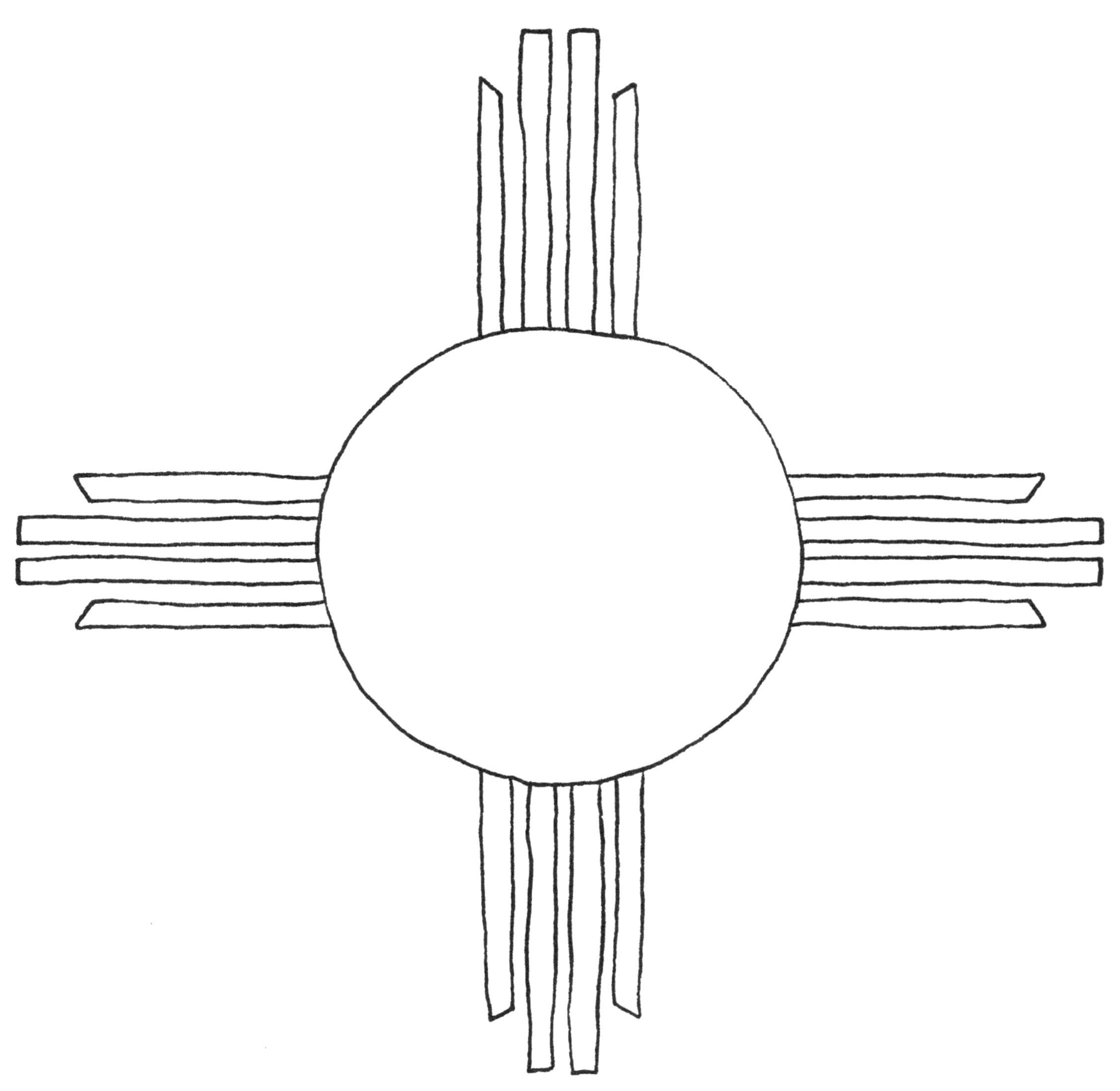

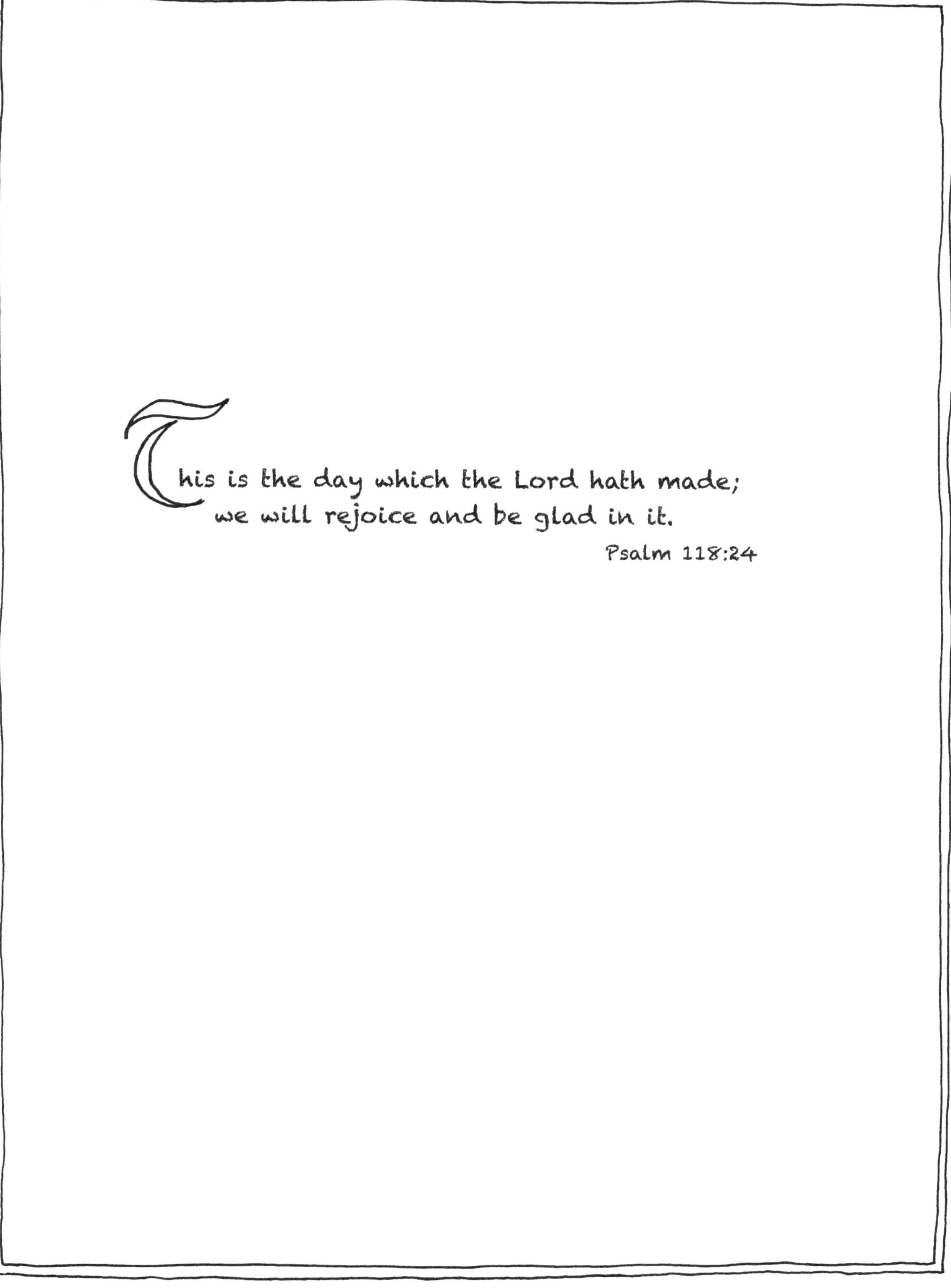
This is the day which the Lord hath made;
we will rejoice and be glad in it.
Psalm 118:24

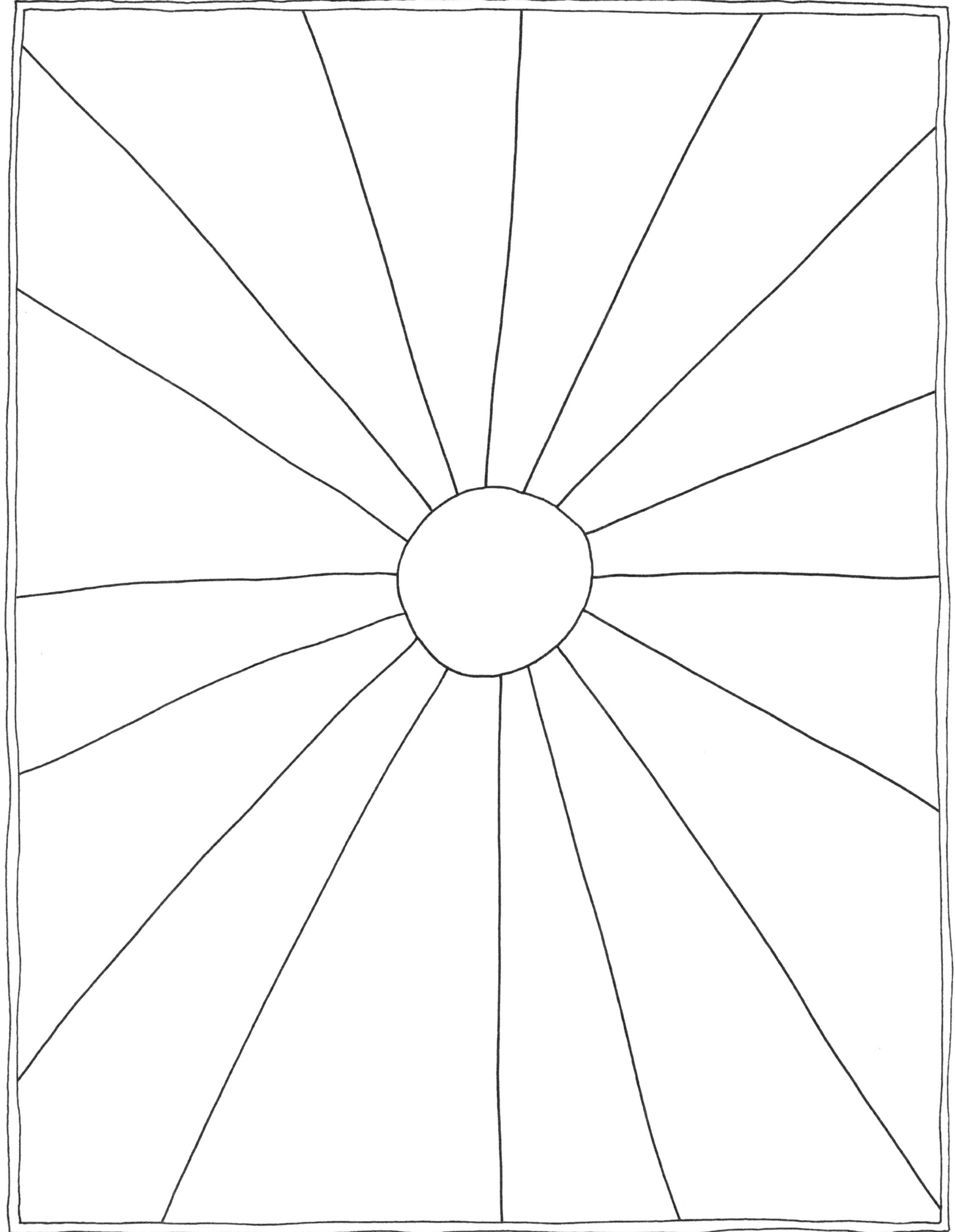

Very early I knew that the only
object in life was to grow.

Margaret Fuller

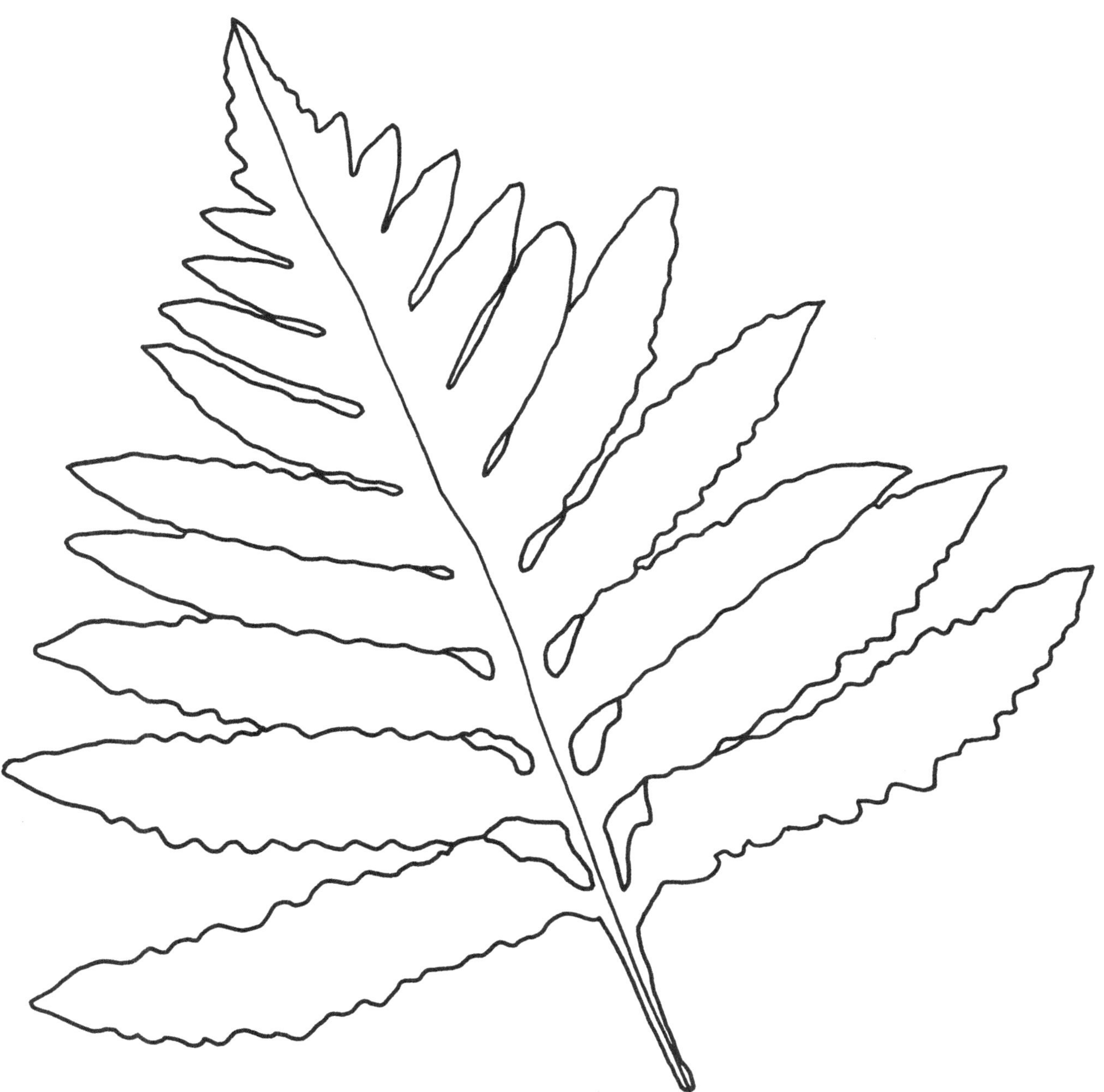

You must live in the present,
launch yourself on every wave,
find your eternity in each moment.

Henry David Thoreau

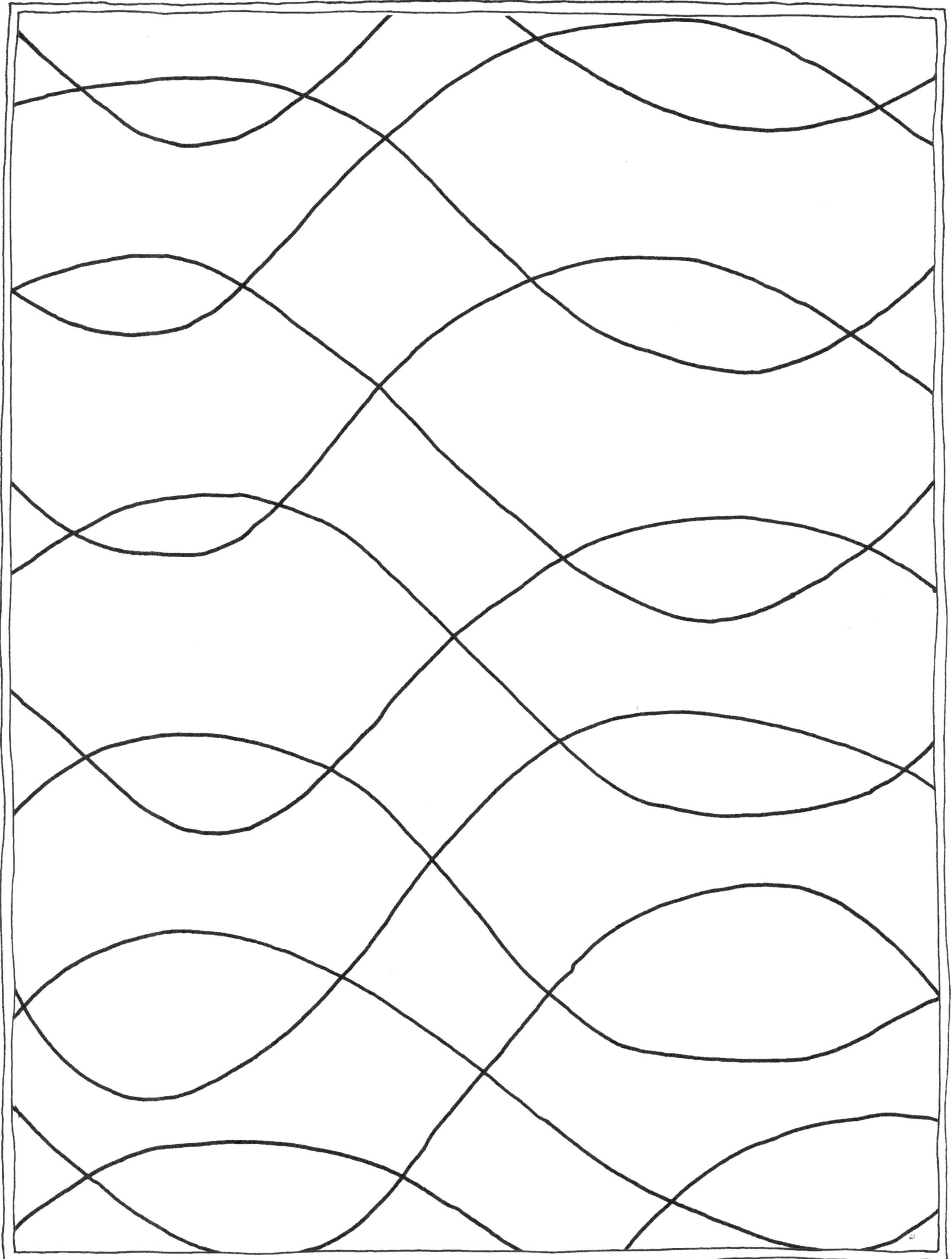

One head (or person) does not hold council.

Akan Proverb (Ghana)

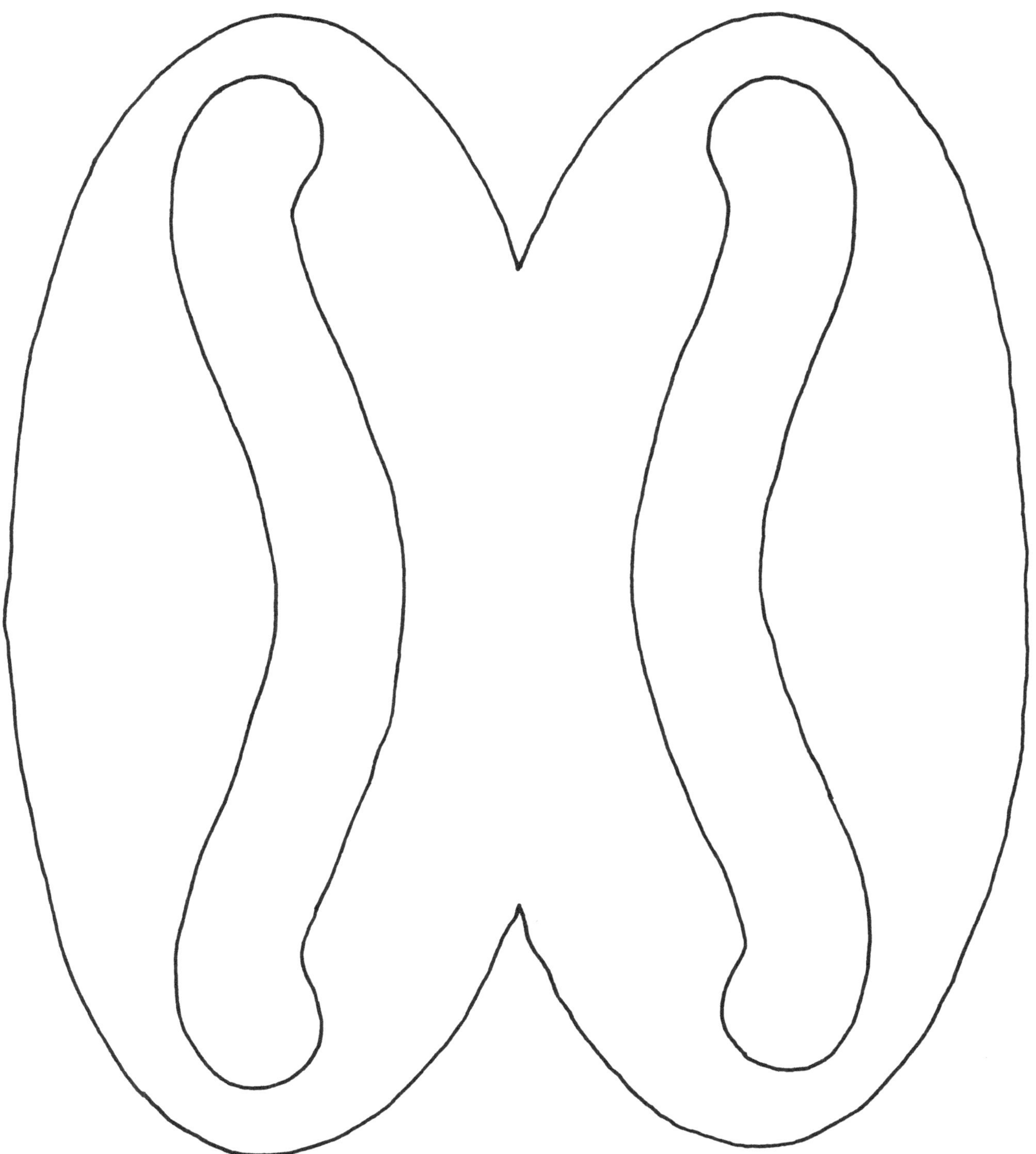

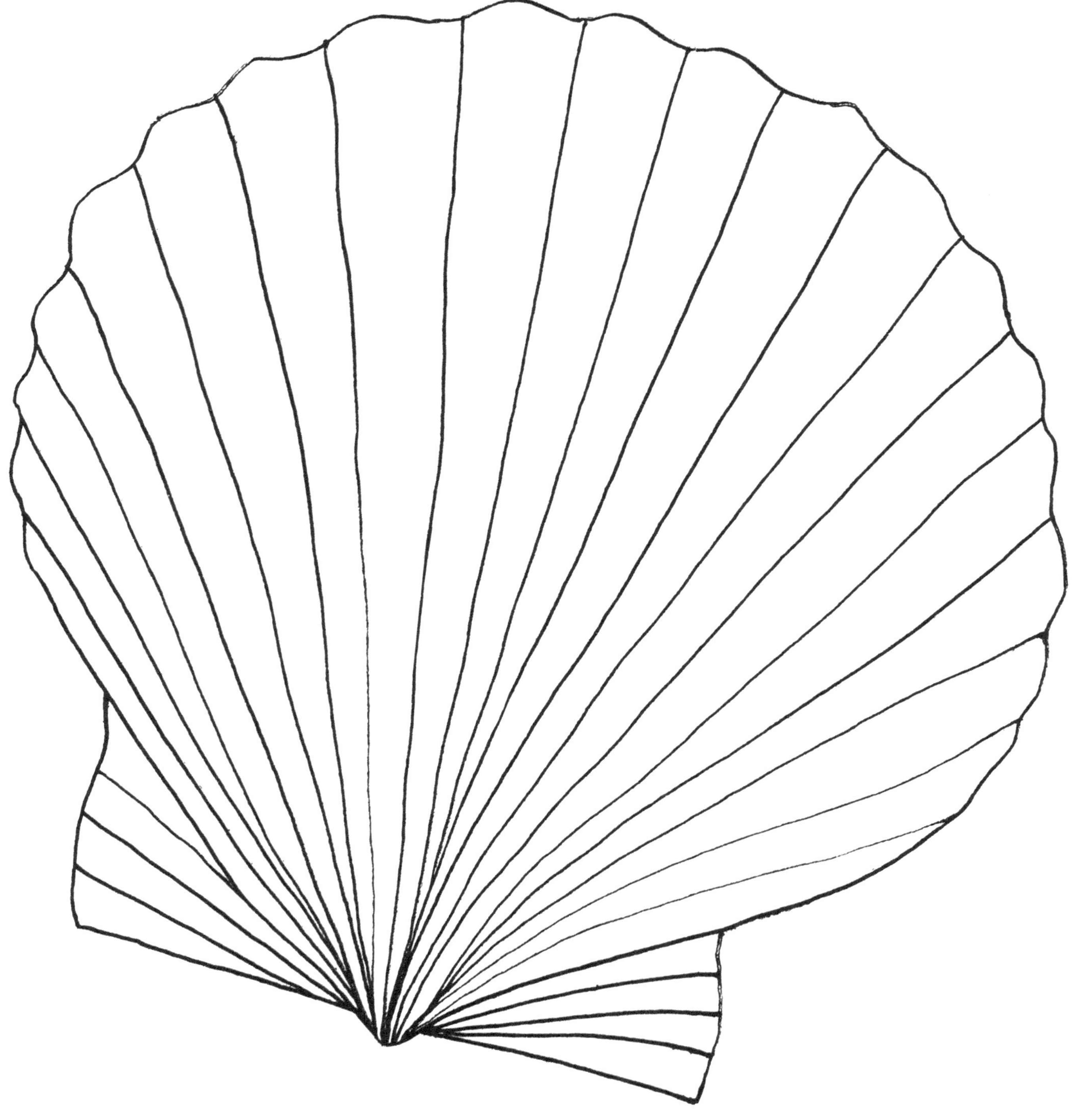

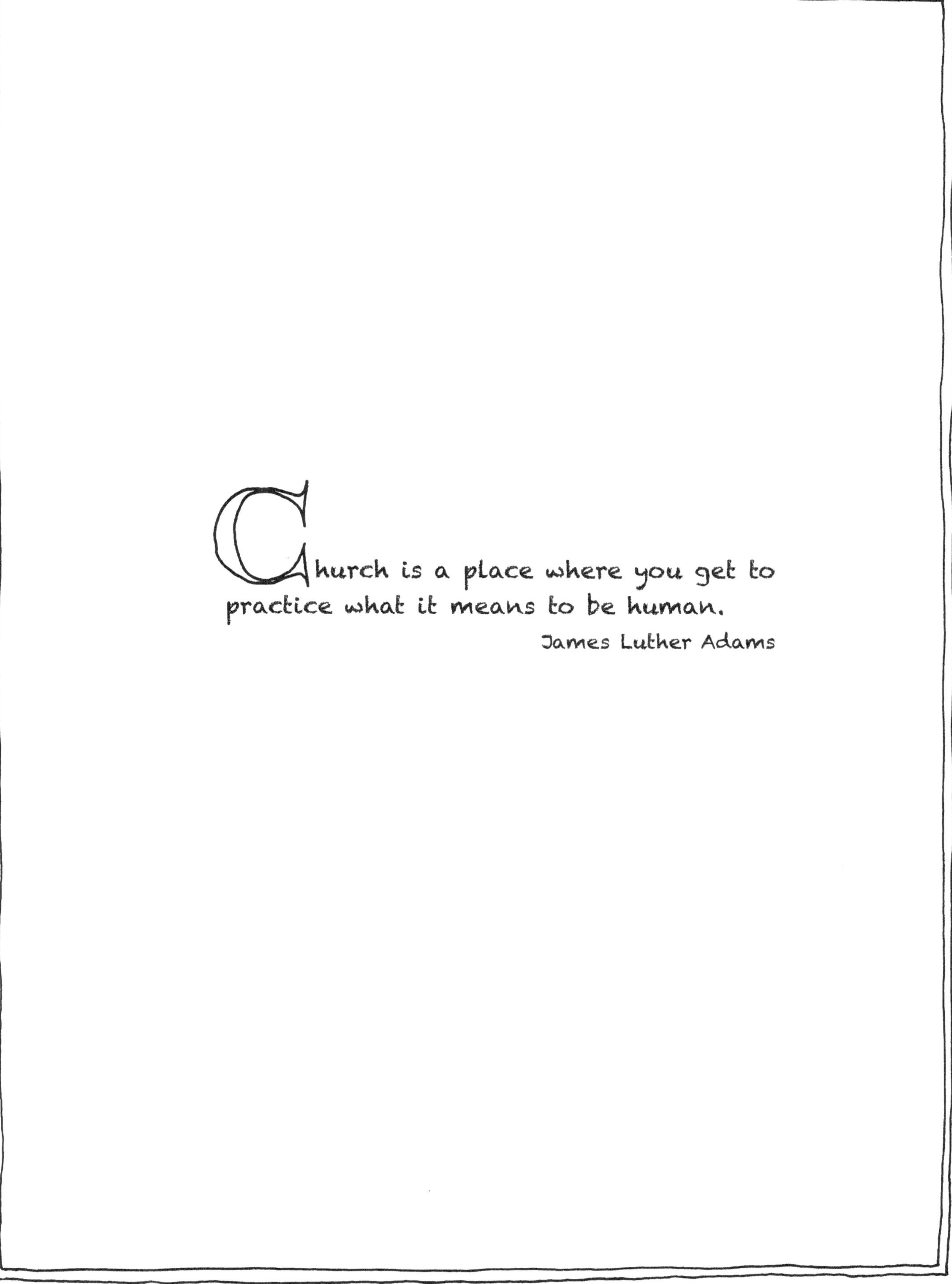

Church is a place where you get to practice what it means to be human.

James Luther Adams

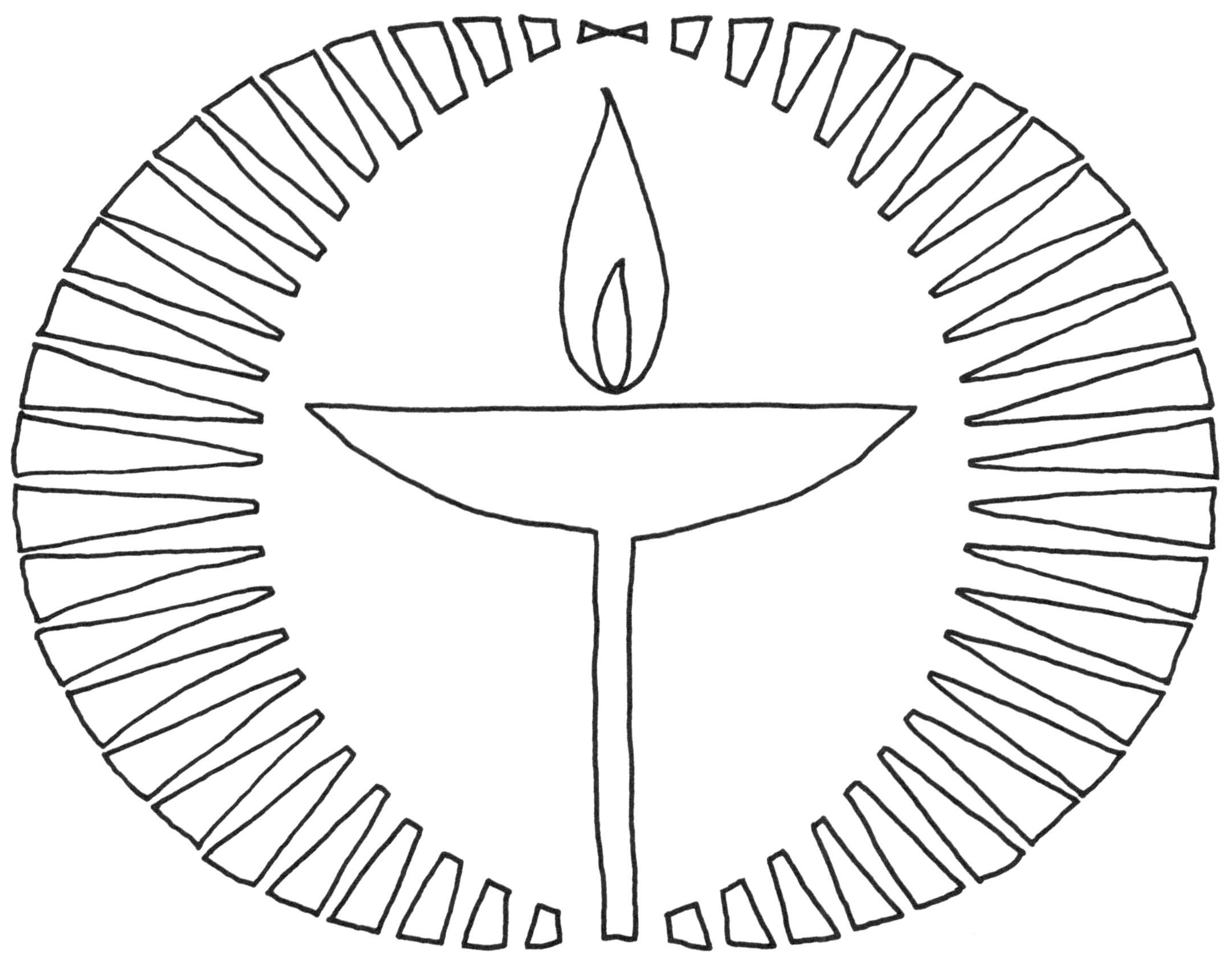

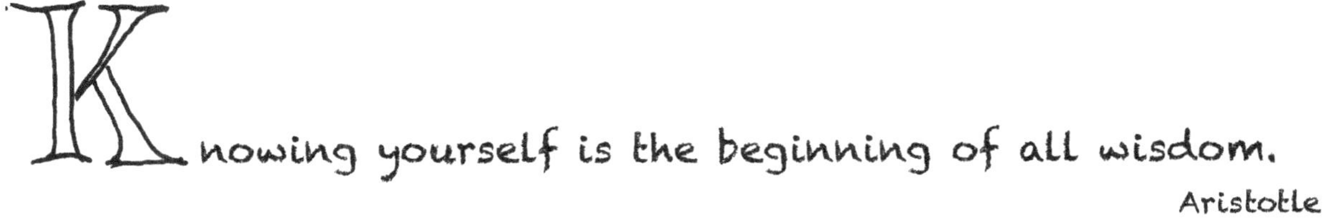
Knowing yourself is the beginning of all wisdom.
Aristotle

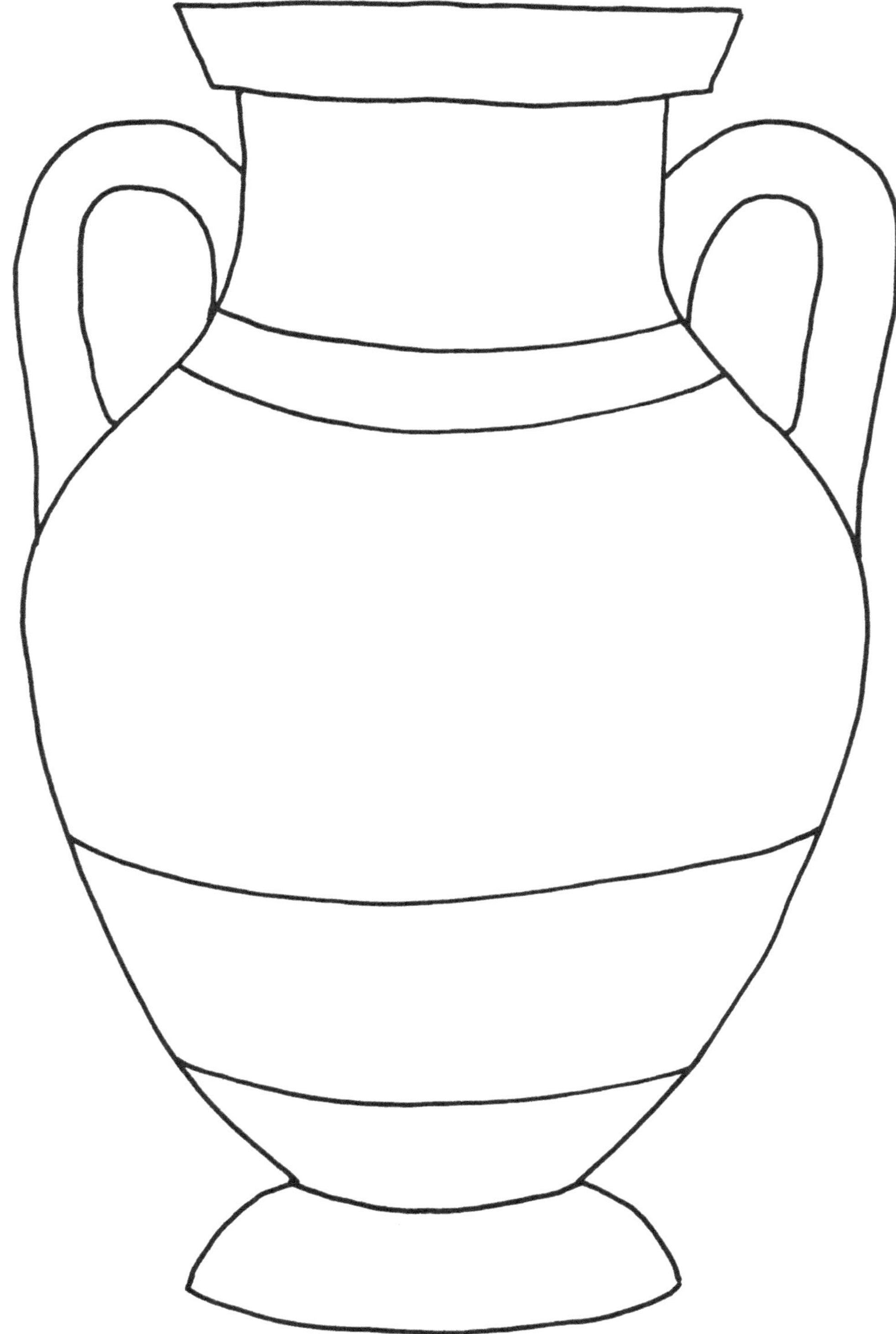

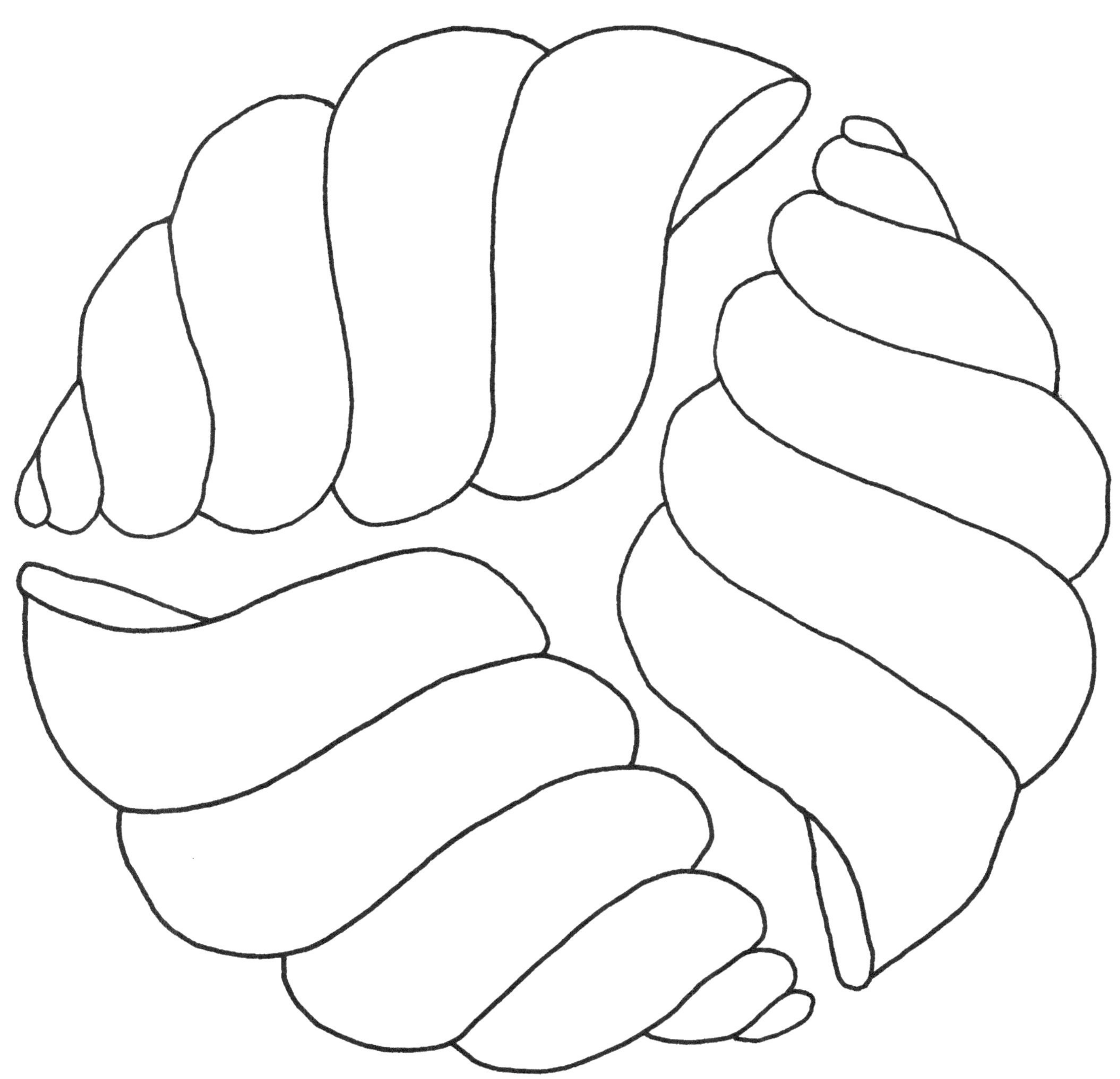

For everything there is a season, and a time for every matter under heaven:
a time to be born, and a time to die;
a time to plant, and a time to pluck up what is planted;
a time to kill, and a time to heal;
a time to break down, and a time to build up;
a time to weep, and a time to laugh;
a time to mourn, and a time to dance.

Ecclesiastes 3:1-4

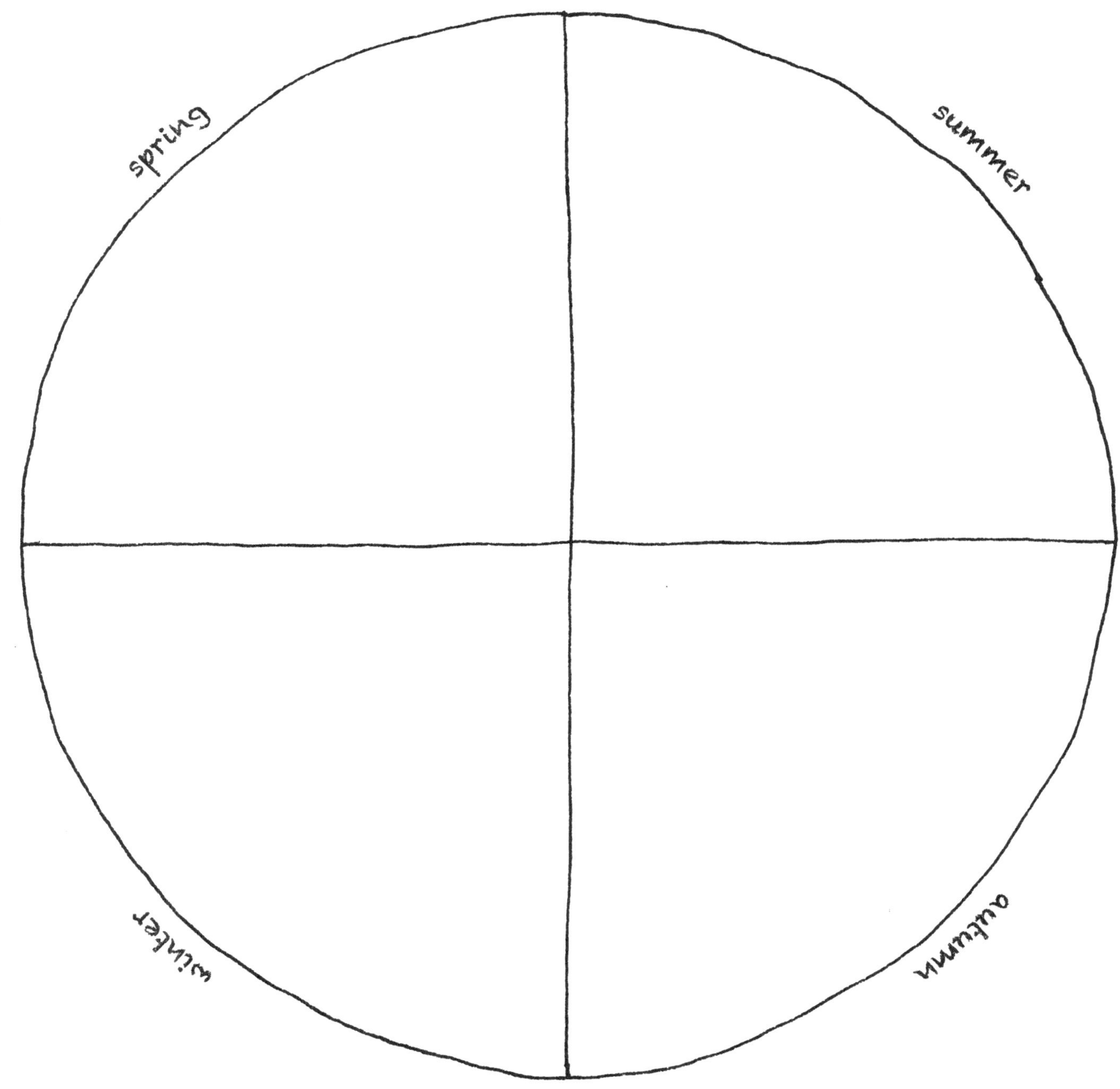

spring
summer
winter
autumn

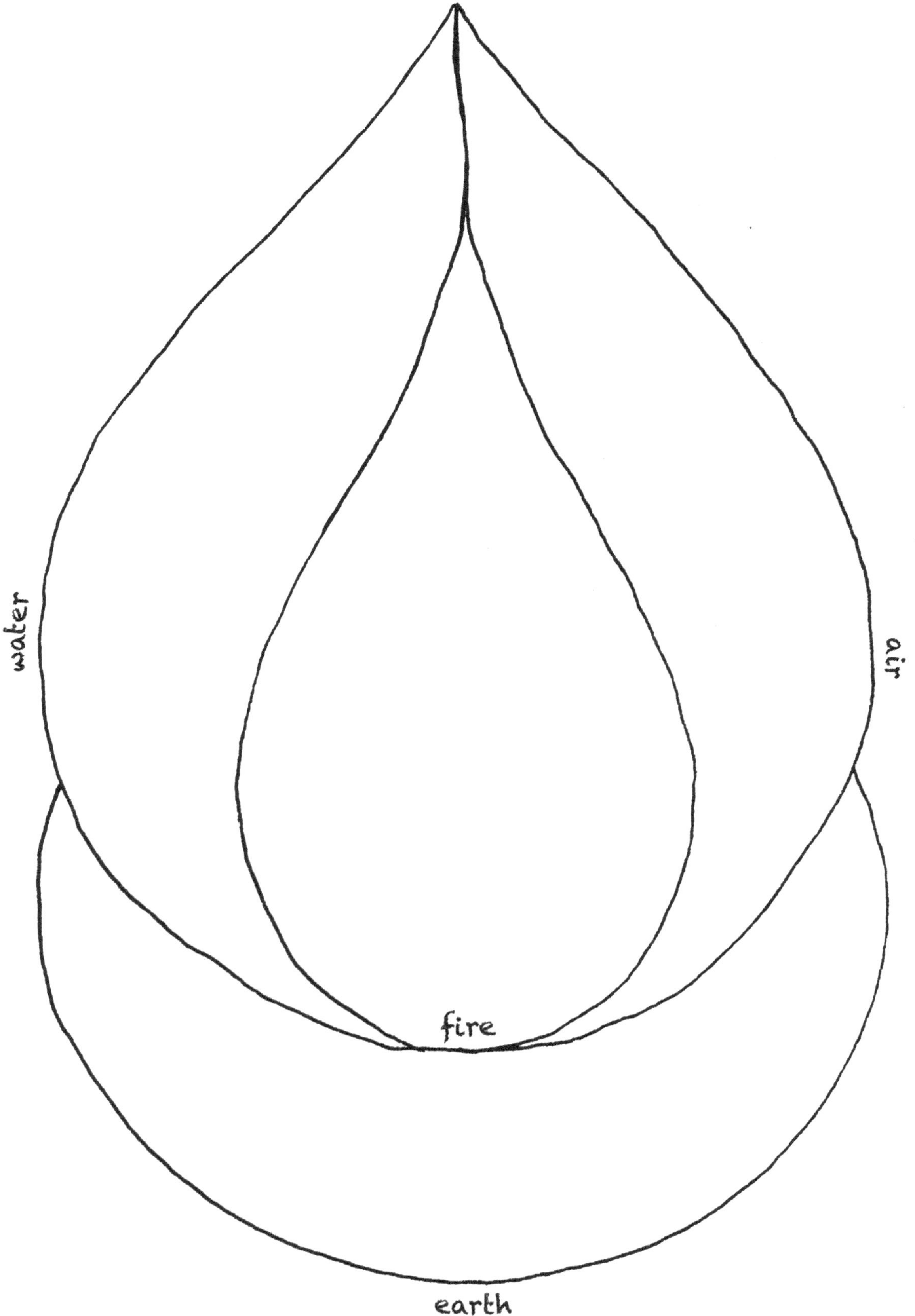

water
air
fire
earth

If you want the truth, I'll tell you the truth.
Listen to the secret sound, the real sound,
which is inside you.

Kabir

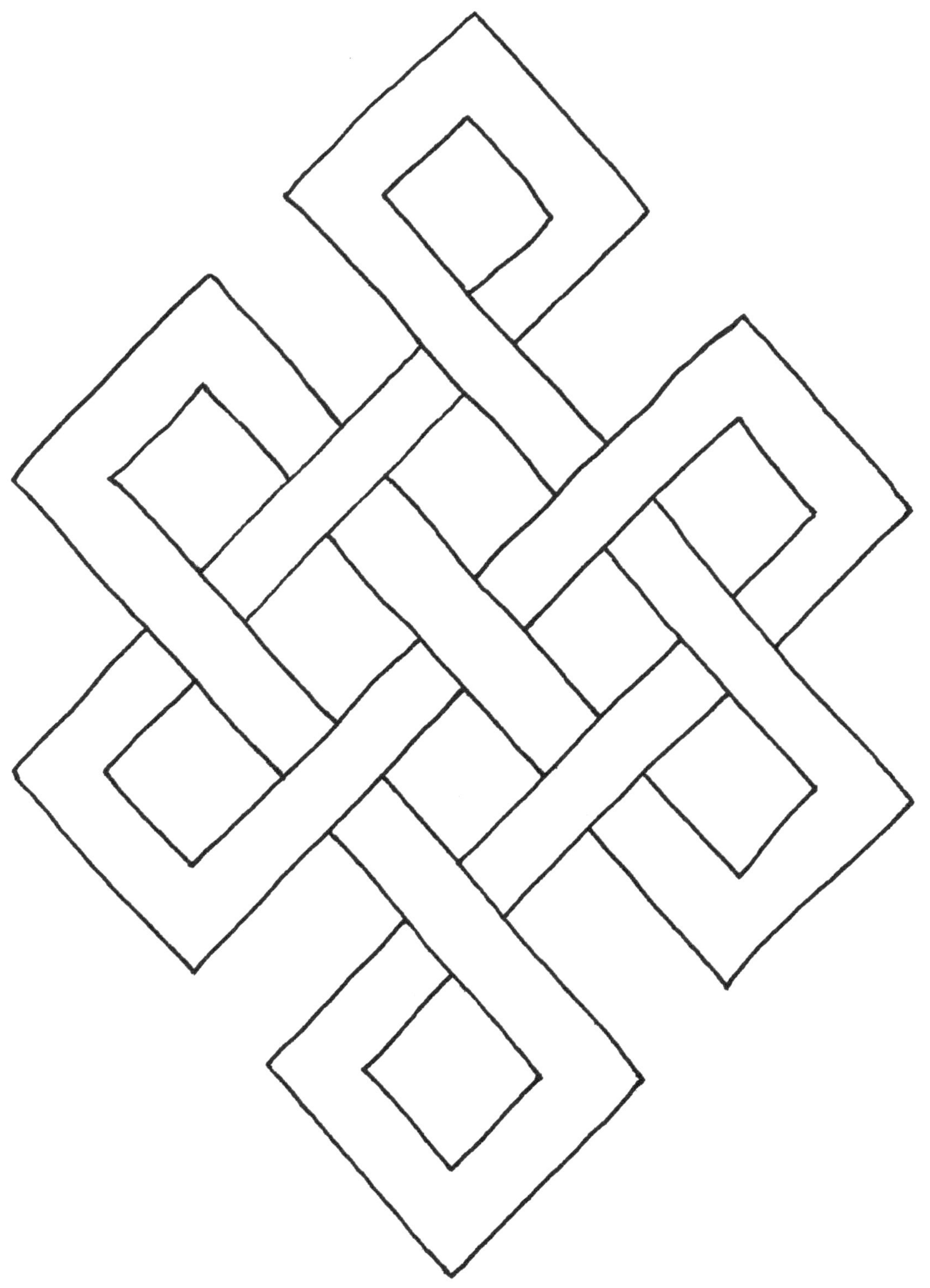

To see the world in a grain of sand
   And heaven in a wild flower
To hold infinity in the palm of your hand
And eternity in an hour.

William Blake

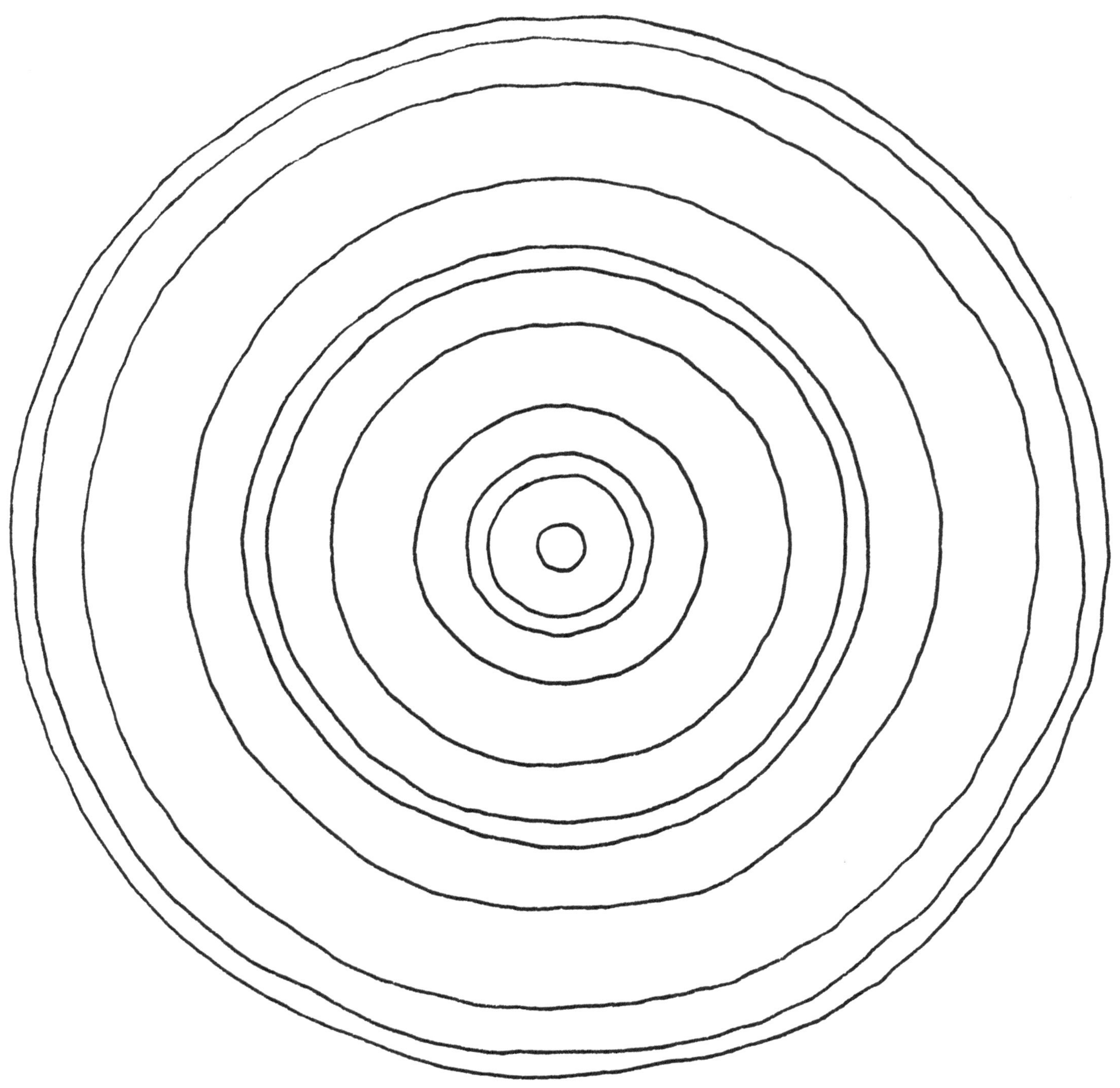

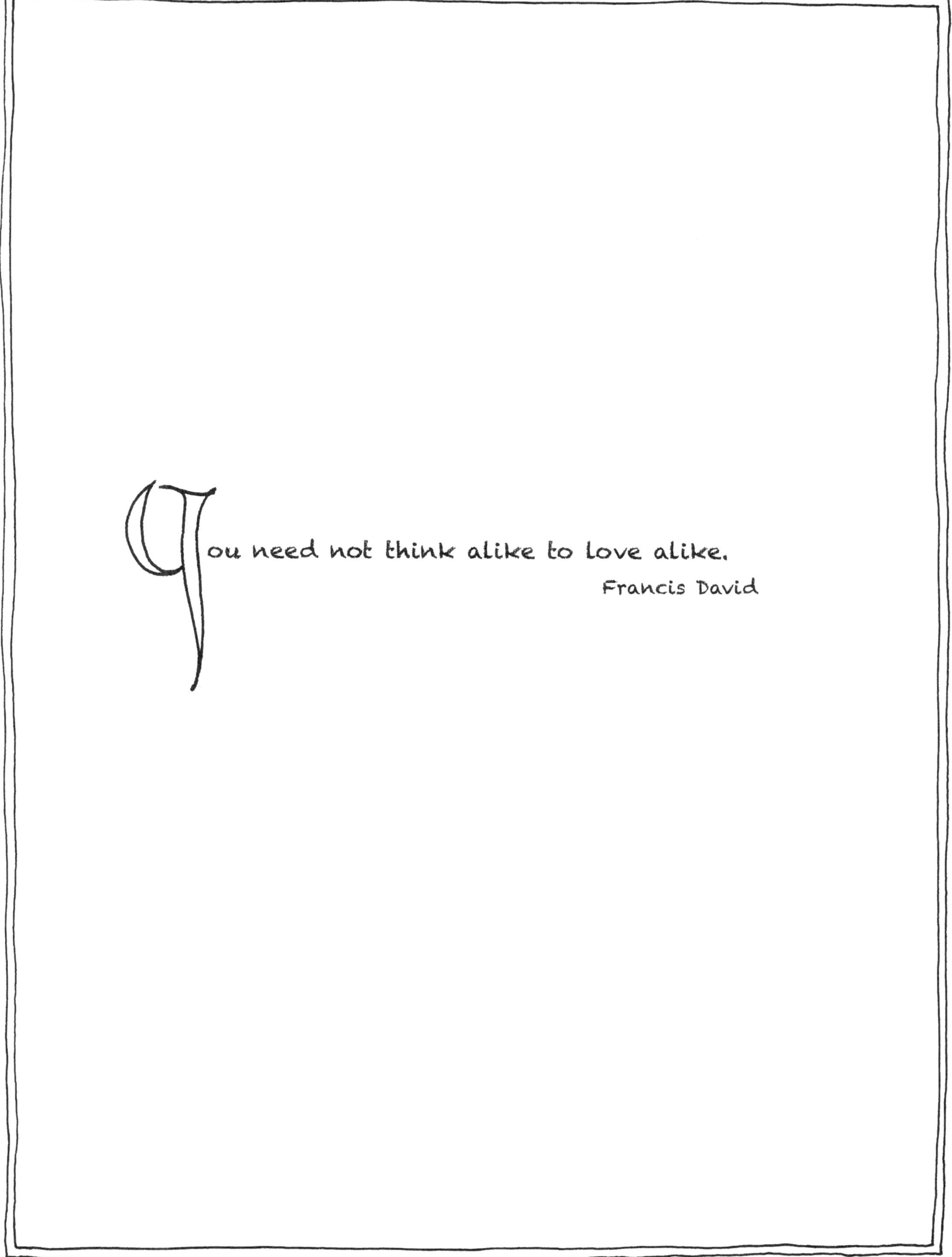

You need not think alike to love alike.

Francis David

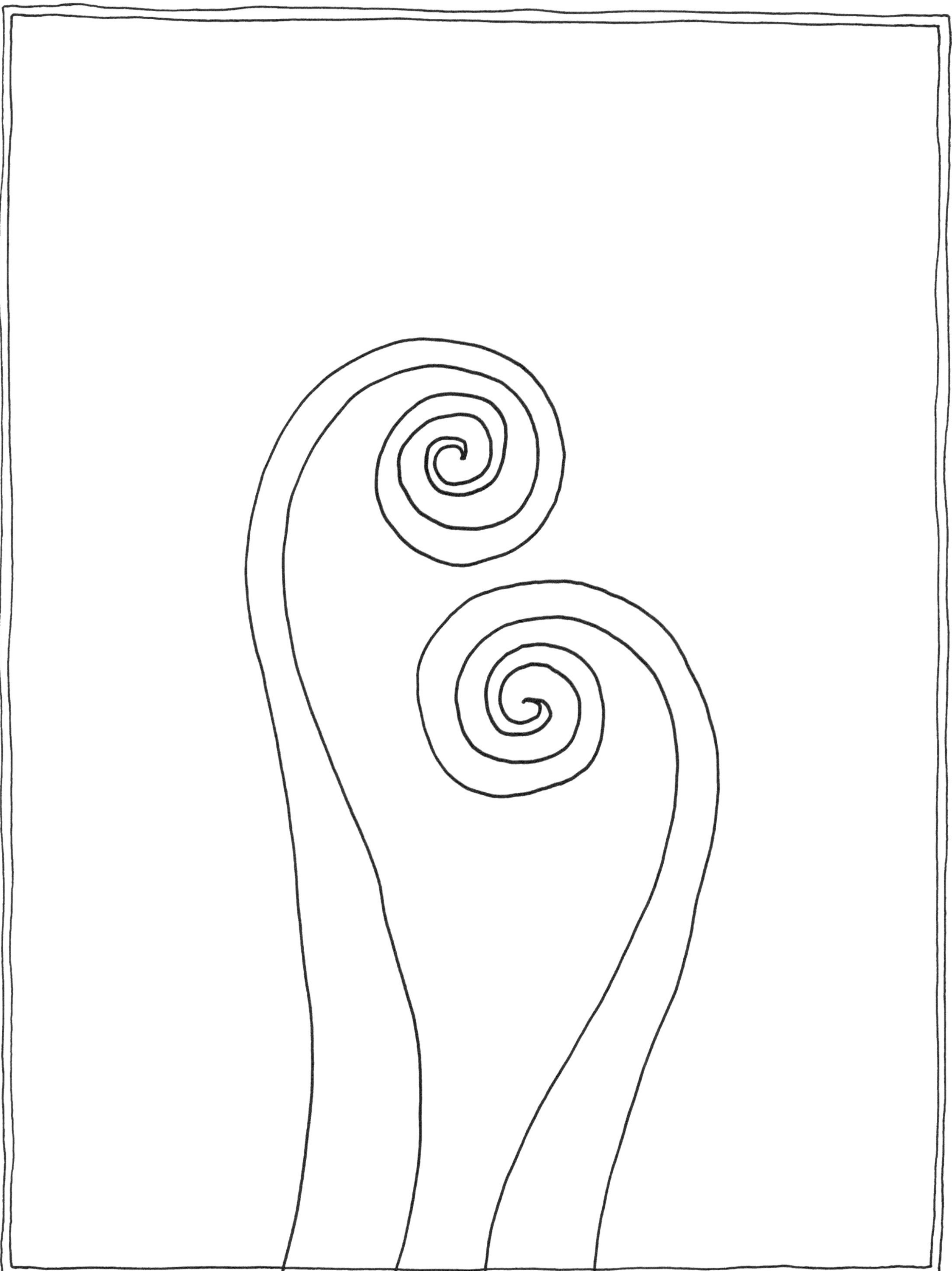

Each of us is meant to have a character
all our own, to be what no other can exactly be,
and do what no other can exactly do.

William Ellery Channing

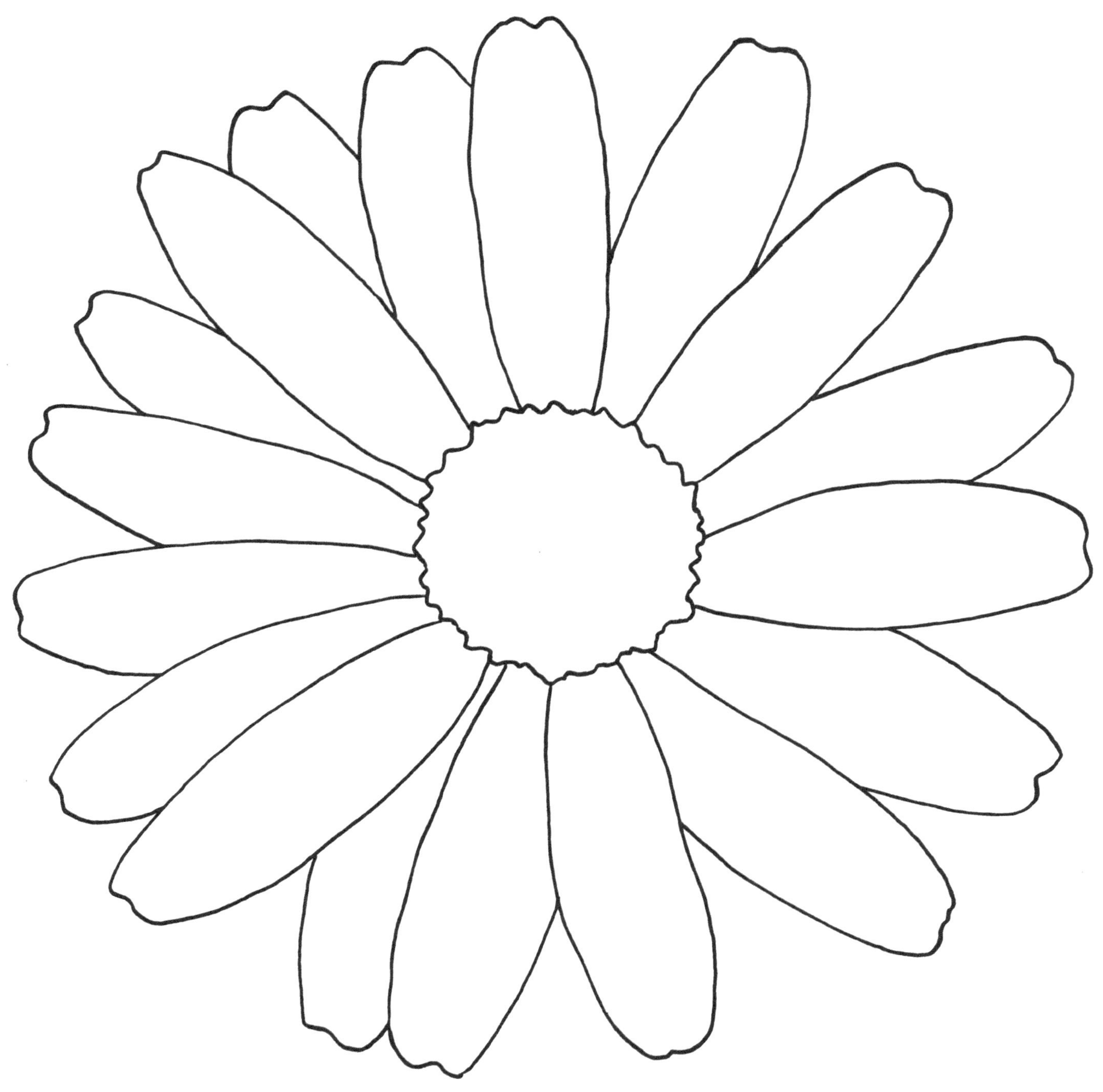

We are all visitors to this time, this place.
We are just passing through. Our purpose here is
to observe, to learn, to grow, to love... and then
we return home.

Aboriginal proverb

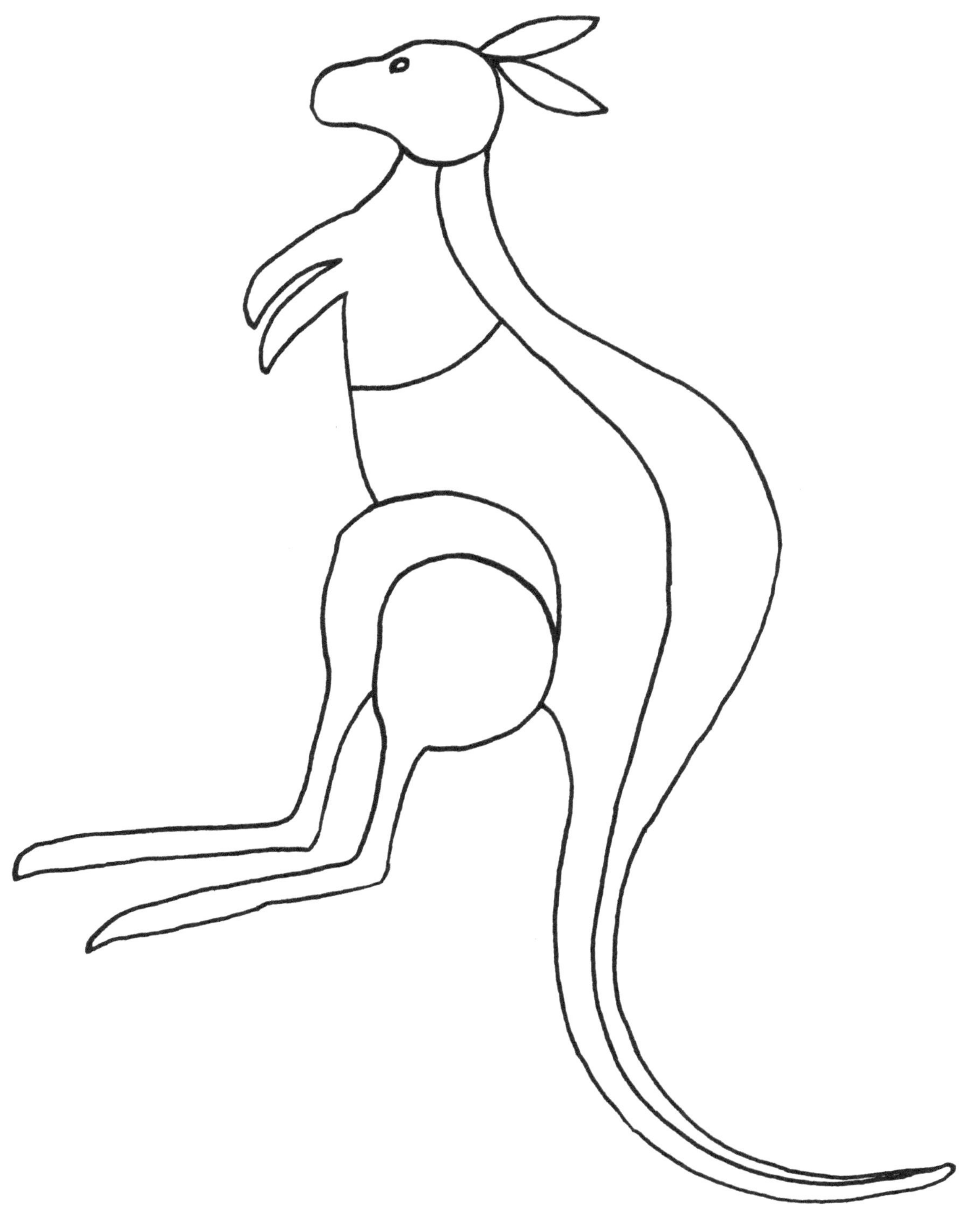

$$L$$ove is the whole thing.
We are only pieces.   Rumi

I offer you peace.
I offer you love.
I offer you friendship.
I see your beauty.
I hear your need.
I feel your feelings.
My wisdom flows from the highest source.
I salute that source in you.
Let us work together.
For unity and peace.
Mahatma Gandhi

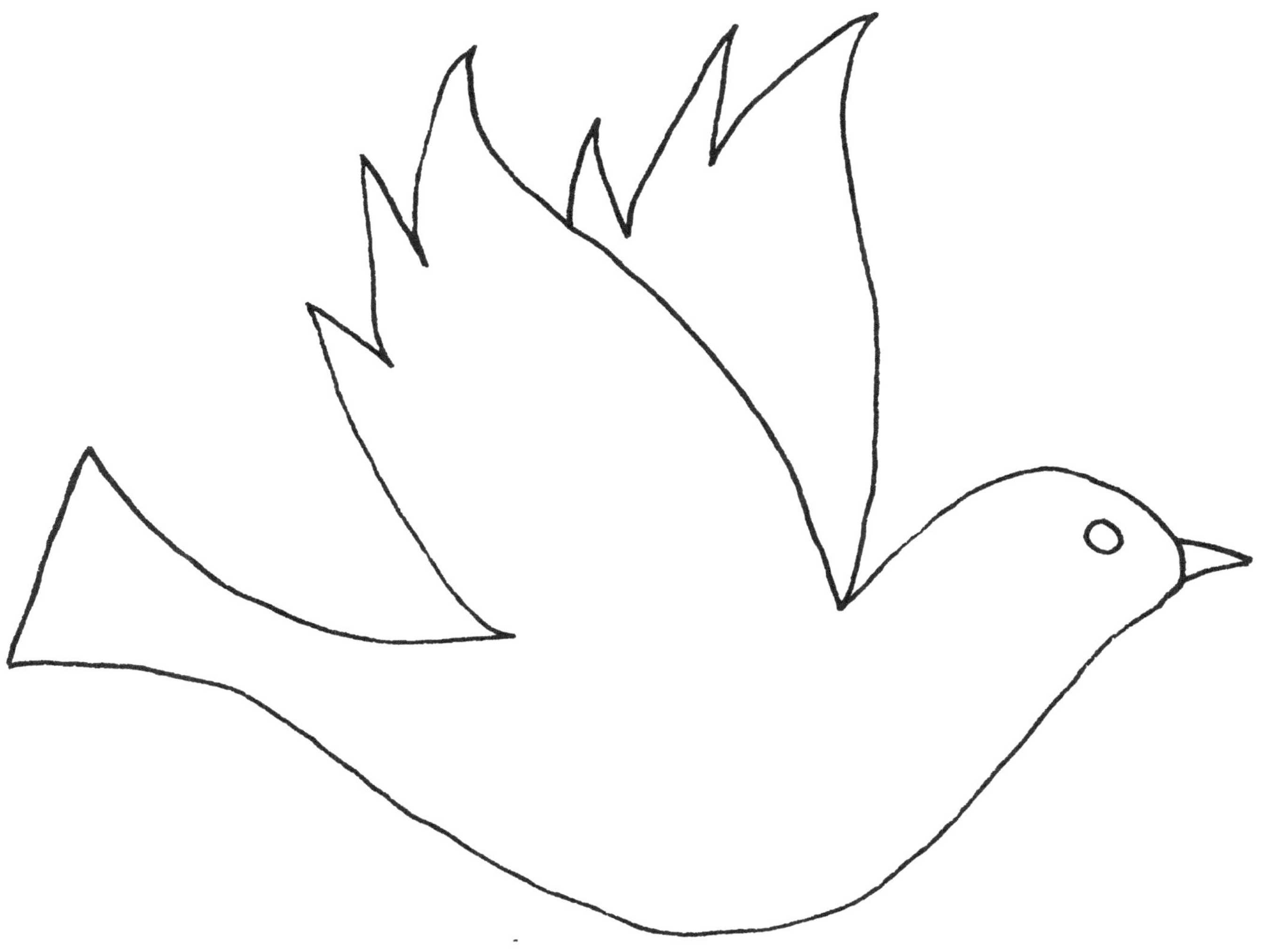

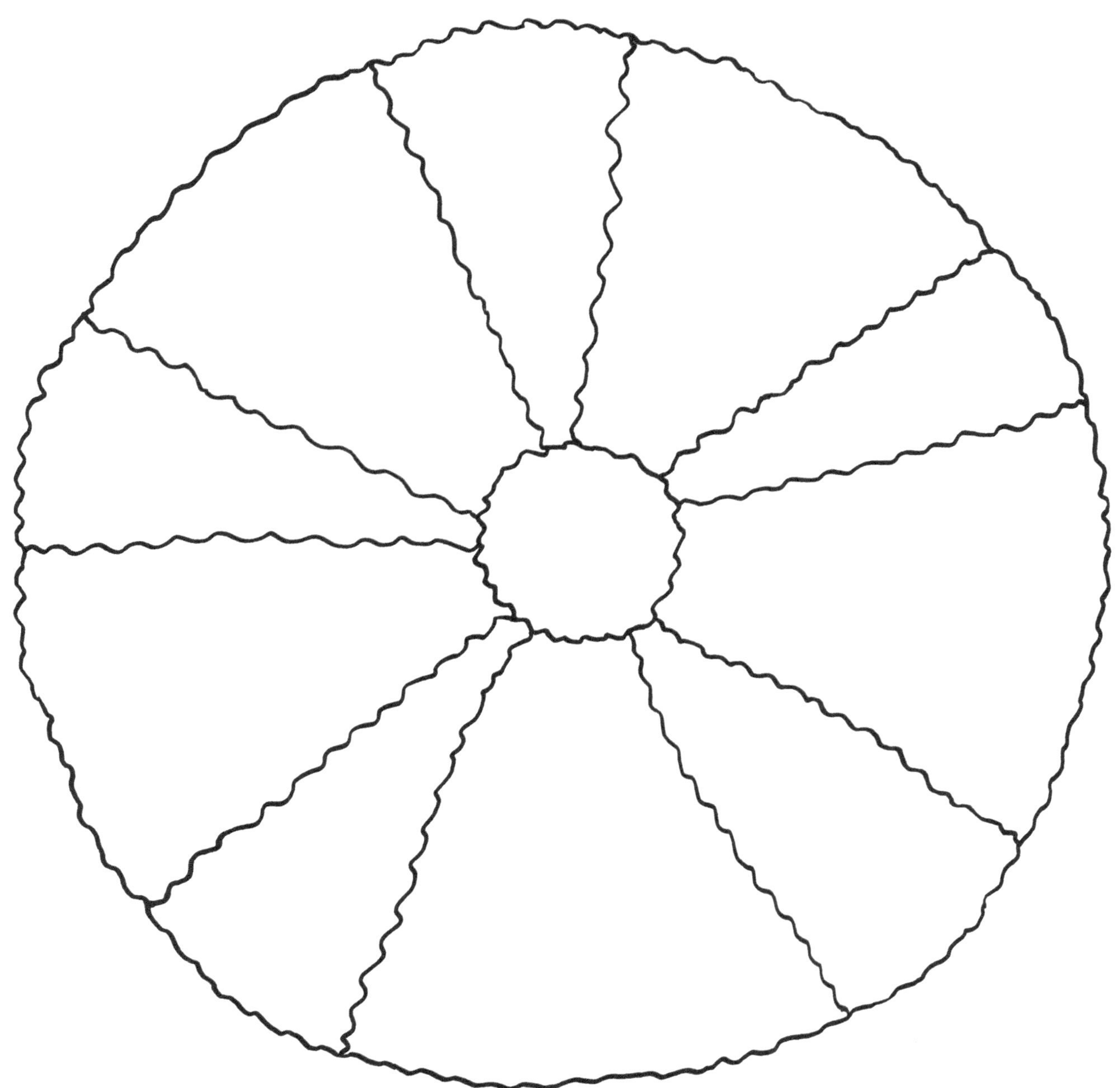

I'm not afraid of storms,
for I'm learning how to sail my ship.
Louisa May Alcott

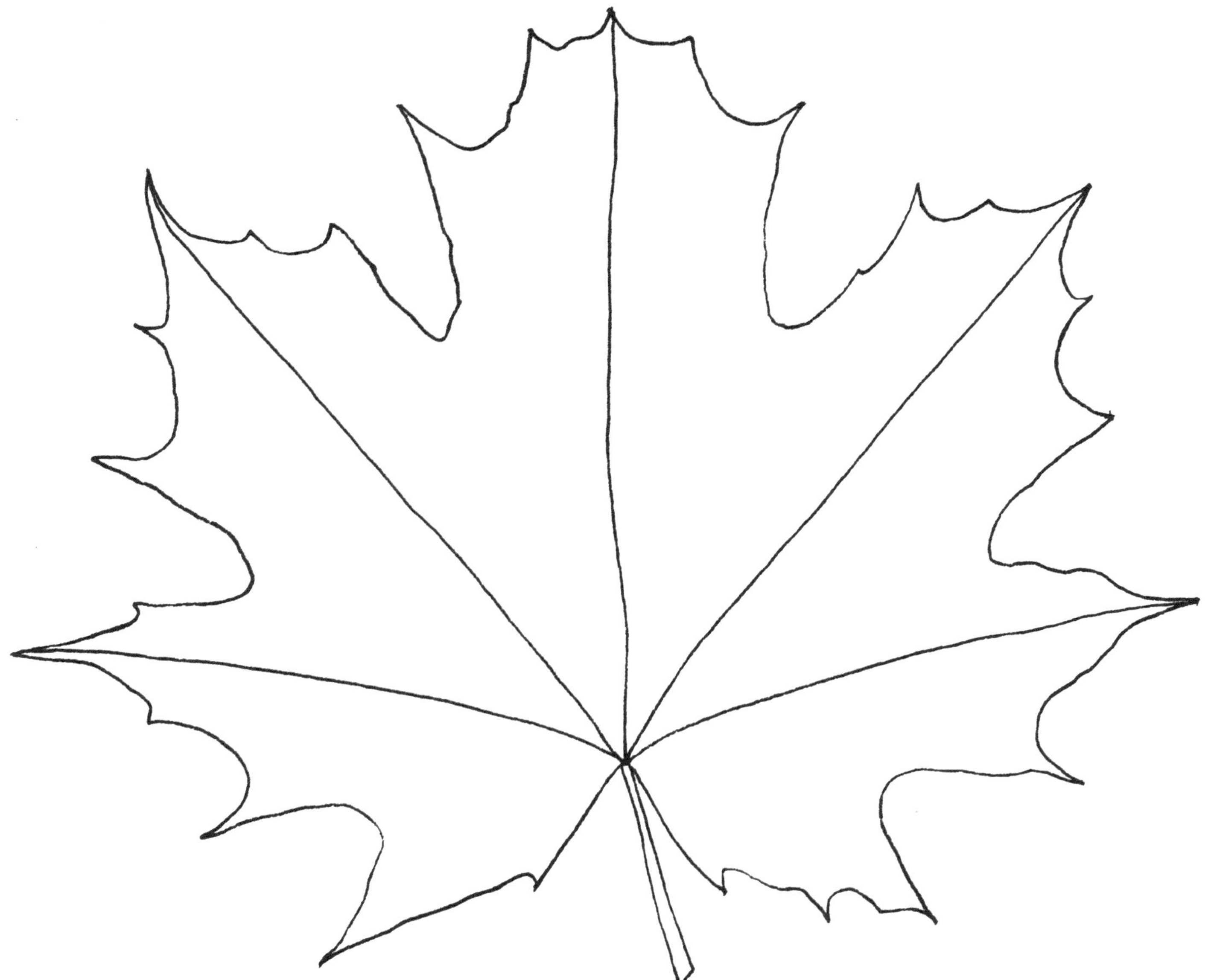

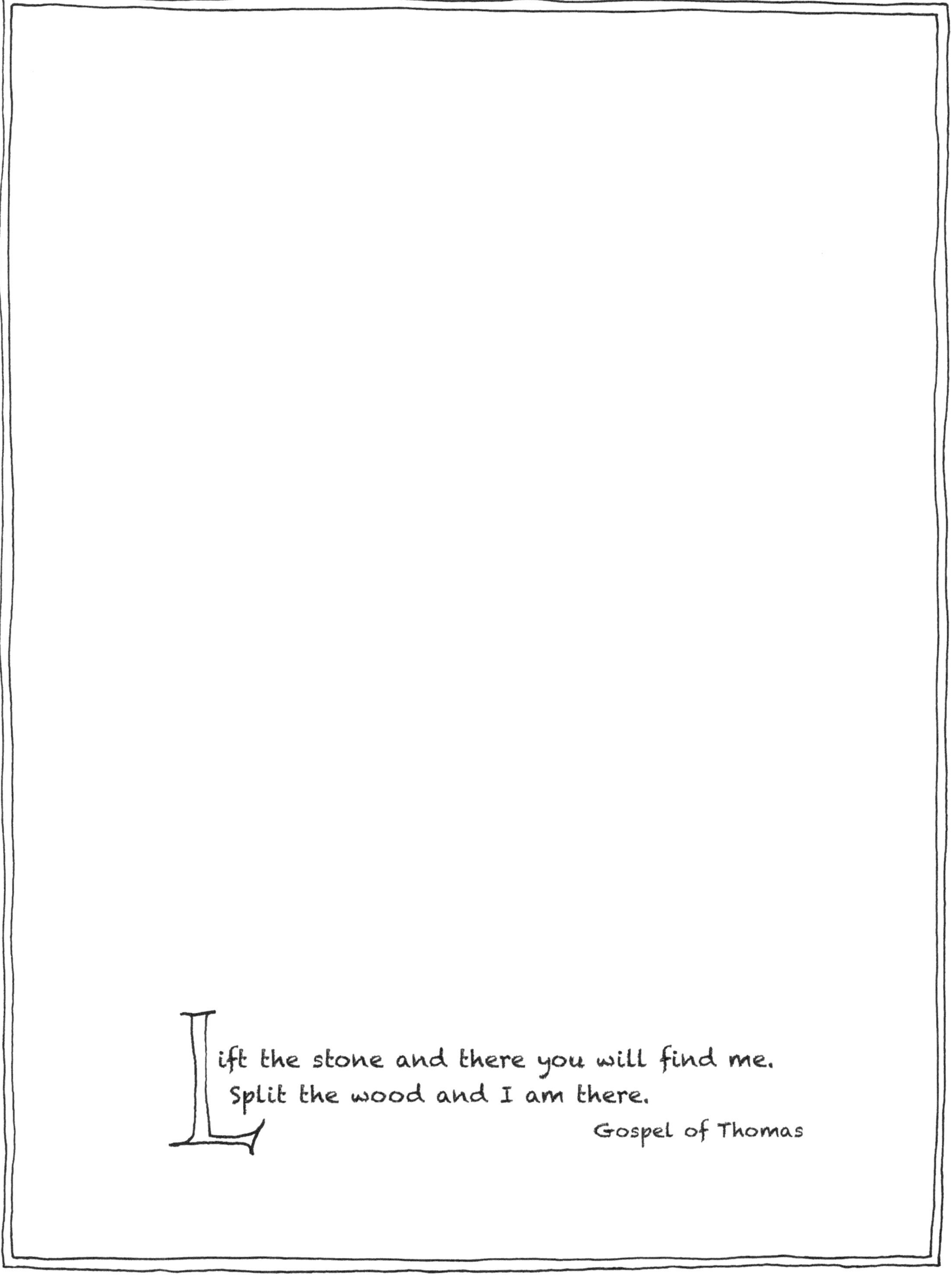

Lift the stone and there you will find me.
Split the wood and I am there.

Gospel of Thomas

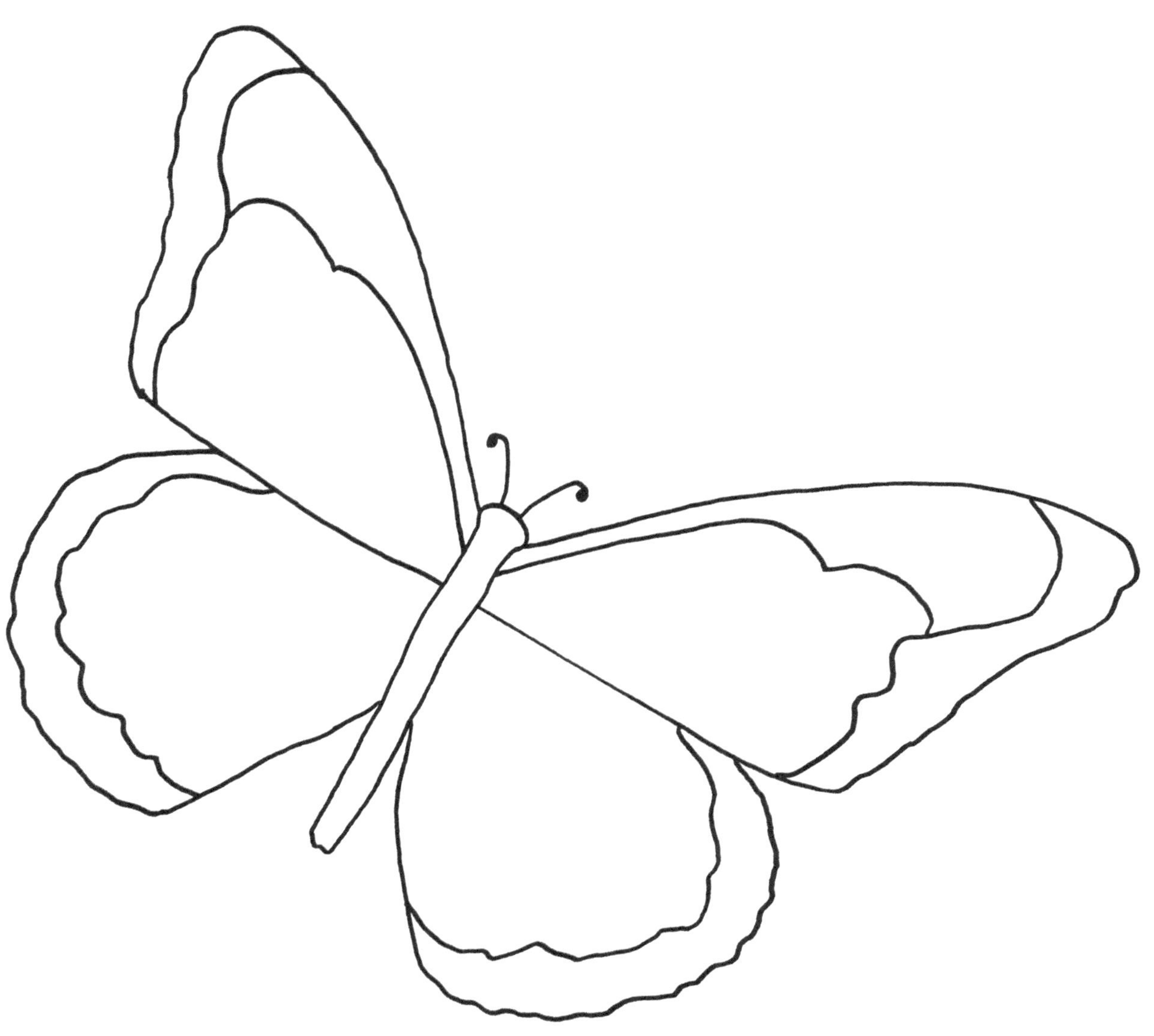

I believe in God, only I spell it Nature.
Frank Lloyd Wright

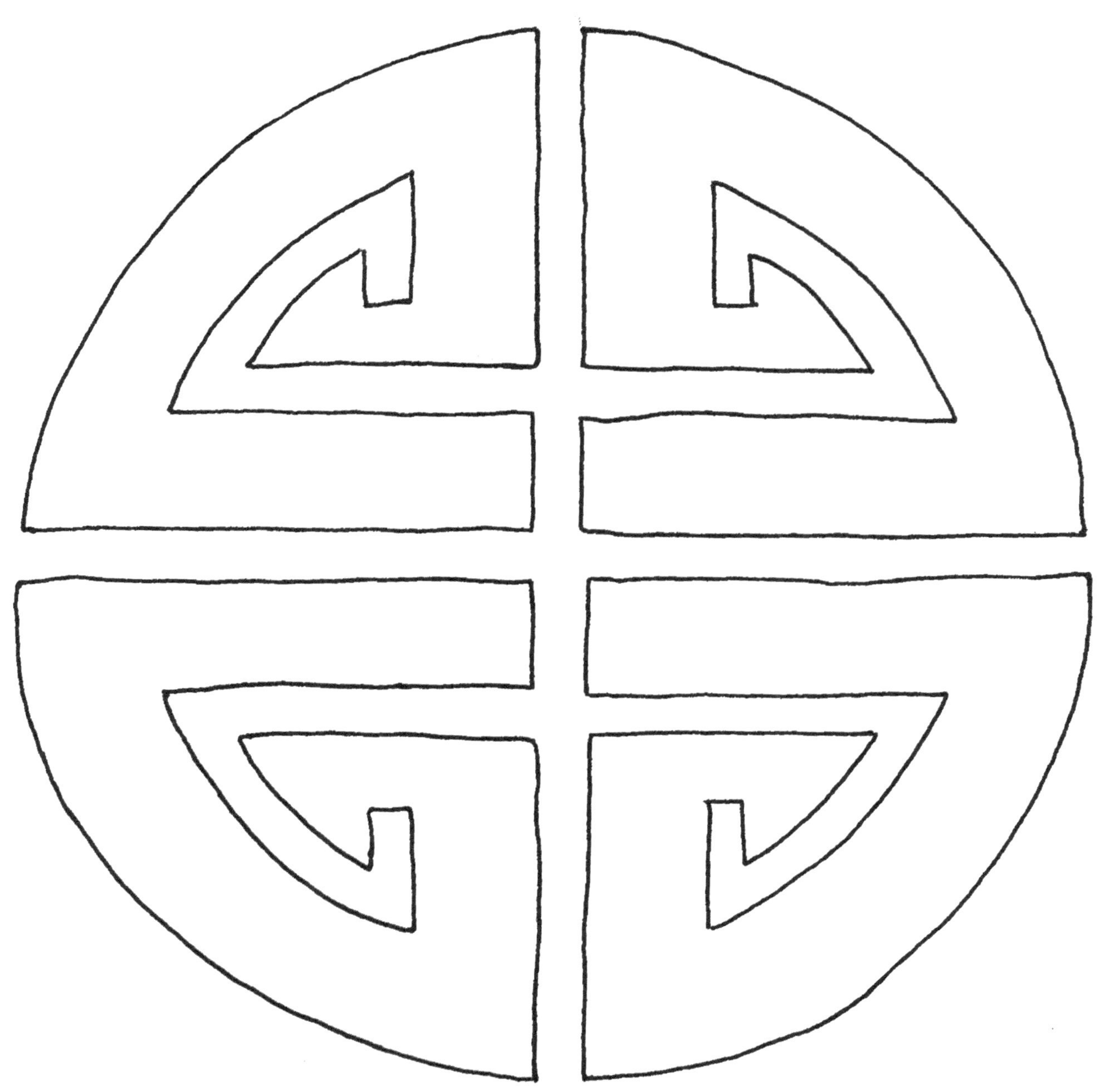

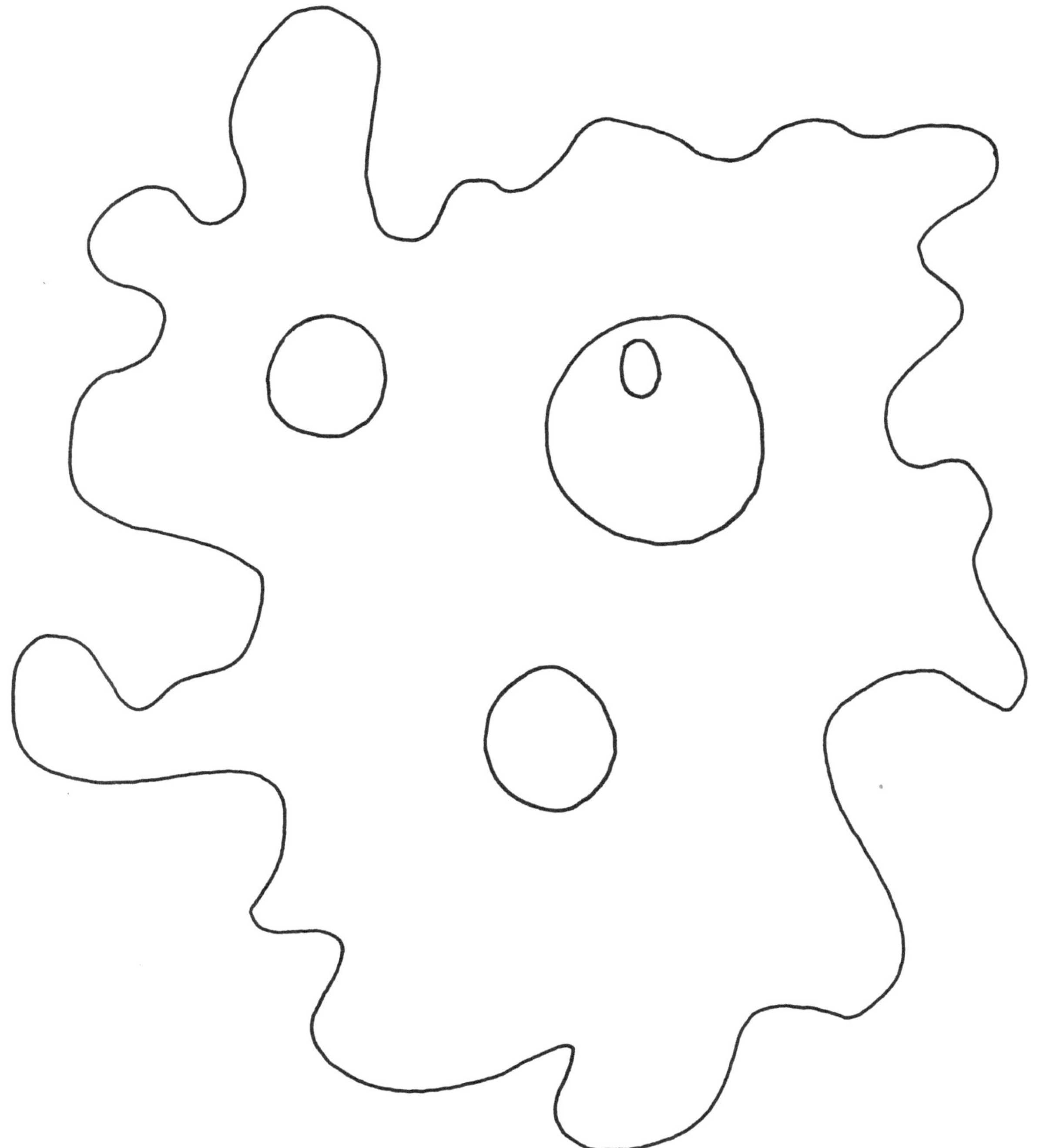

I defy the tyranny of precedent. I cannot afford the luxury of a closed mind. I go for anything new that might improve the past.

Clara Barton

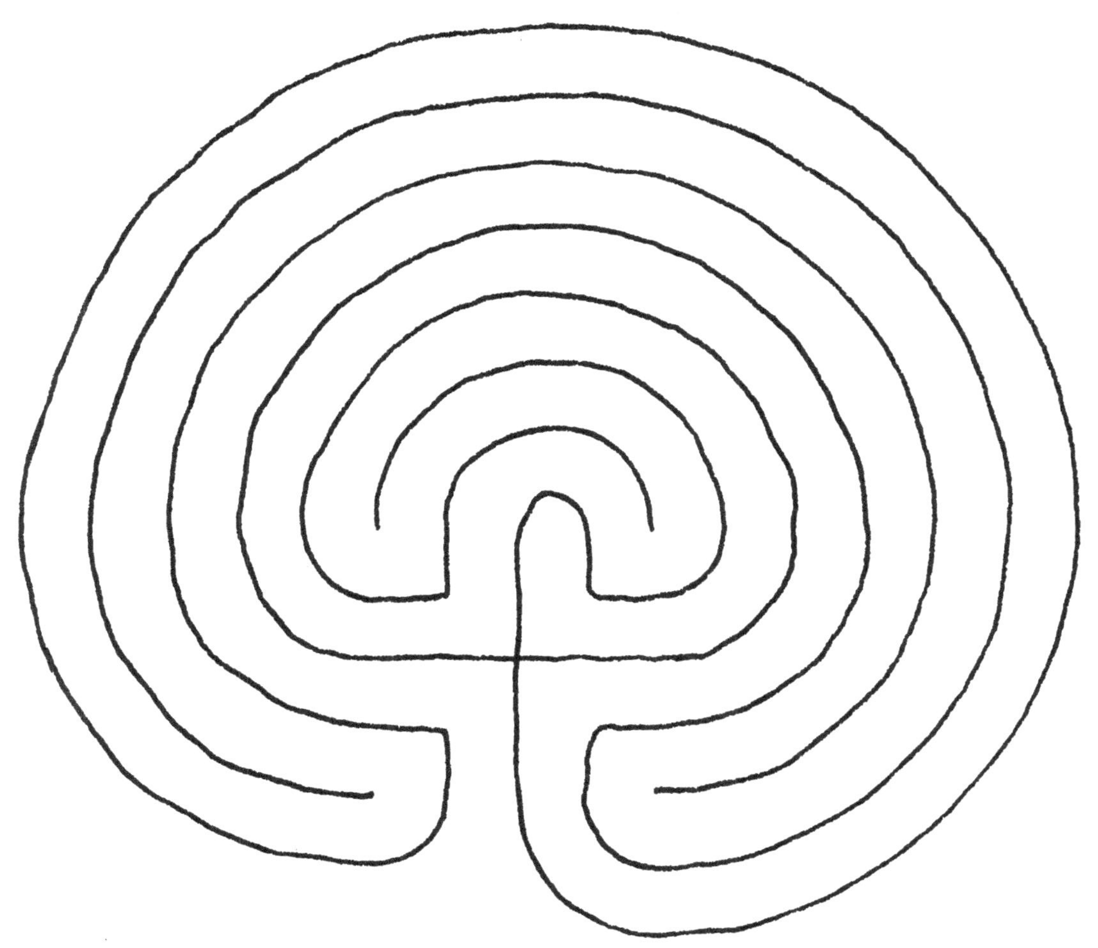

Here is information about where the quotes and pictures I used came from:

Sources of the quotes: I have tried hard to be sure that the quotes in this journal are accurate and from the book or source I say they are from. I think this is important, not only because that's what's fair to the person who said or wrote it, but because that way, if you read something you find interesting, you can look up the person or the source and find out more. Same goes for the outlines.

Sources of the outlines:

www.ingramcontent.com/pod-product-compliance
Lightning Source LLC
Chambersburg PA
CBHW080358030726
47598CB00010B/2803